THE NEGRO CHURCH
IN AMERICA

SOURCEBOOKS IN NEGRO HISTORY

The Negro Church in America

E. FRANKLIN FRAZIER

SCHOCKEN BOOKS · NEW YORK

Preface

THE sudden and most untimely death of Franklin Frazier has compelled us to accept the necessity to publish this volume as a tribute to his memory. It will be found to be a valuable addition to his works, dealing with a subject of great intrinsic importance, written (as was always the case with Professor Frazier's books) with sympathy and insight, and in the most lucid and attractive prose. The volume starts with an appreciation of his achievements by his colleague and friend, Professor Everett Hughes. All who were privileged to know Professor Frazier will be grateful to Professor Hughes for his tribute, and will appreciate its warmth.

T. S. SIMEY

E. Franklin Frazier

A MEMOIR BY EVERETT C. HUGHES

FRANKLIN Frazier, by a sort of genius for essentials, devoted his career mainly to the study of two American institutions, the Negro family and the Negro church. Barred from full and equal participation in any of the public institutions of the country and not permitted to develop their own in most realms of life, American Negroes were 'free'—in an ironic sense—to develop their own family and religious life. By American caste rule, no person of any degree of known Negro ancestry can be 'kin' to any person supposedly of no such ancestry. Negro Americans had to make their own family institutions. White Americans, who became white because they had black slaves, having made Christians of their field hands, did not want to commune with them from the same cup. Hence at birth, confirmation, communion, marriage, death and all the great turning points and festivals, Negro and white were alien to each other. The separation was not quite reciprocal. Negroes were often spectators, and more, of the intimate life of whites, while the whites—although they had no shame about intruding—saw little of the intimate life of Negroes. Religion and family became foci of Negro life in a special degree.

But the story of the American Negro family and church has been told by Frazier himself. Let me talk of the man. He studied with Robert E. Park at the University of Chicago. Now Park, although intensely interested in the social attitudes of which his colleague William I. Thomas wrote so much, insisted that the psychology of race, or of anything else, be studied in whole ecological and social settings. He set us, his students, to studying the various kinds of economic, political and social arrangements which grew up where races and nations met and especially where one had great power over another. I did not know Frazier before he had studied with Park, but certainly the toughness and subtlety of Park's approach came naturally to him. He became our toughest student of race relations; tough on well-meaning whites who tried to escape full responsibility for American racial injustice by inviting nice Negroes to dinner to prove they had no prejudice; tough on all who let condescension creep into their talk or actions; but toughest of all on those American Negroes who used segregation as a wall behind which to hide in a whining, comfortable, snobbish mediocrity. *Black Bourgeoisie*, in which he castigated his fellows, may, as a social and political tract, be Frazier's greatest contribution. Americans of any hue, if they read it well, will wince as they feel his touch in their moral wounds. Nor is *Black Bourgeoisie* only incidentally about *Negro* Americans.

Race and Culture Contacts in the Modern World might also be considered Frazier's best work. But that would be like making a Beethoven symphony compete with a quartet. It is of another *genre*. In it Frazier gives to the academic world the essence of Robert E. Park's system of analysis of racial relations. To one who knew both men well, this book is an organic blend of the thoughts of the two. It is no belittling of Frazier to say that in this book he writes as a disciple; a disciple, well-ripened, who feels no need to deny his debt.

Fortunately Frazier has left us a full sample of his work and thought, from the intimacy of *The Negro Family in the United States*, warmth and liveliness of *The Negro Church in America* and the lashing criticism of *Black Bourgeoisie*, to the historic sweep of *The Negro in the United States* and the world-wide perspective of *Race and Culture in the Modern World*. But he has not left on paper the warm humanity of a man who felt in every fibre the human comedy and the human tragedy—which are one—visited in special degree on Americans of some Negro ancestry.

Contents

Introduction

IN 1953, I had the unexpected honour to be invited to give the Frazer Lecture in Social Anthropology at the University of Liverpool. At the time I was serving as the Chief of the Division of the Applied Social Sciences in the Department of Social Sciences of UNESCO in Paris. The choice of a subject for the Frazer Lecture did not present any special difficulty since it would most appropriately be in the field of religion and I had given some attention to religion in my studies of the American Negro. The main difficulty arose from the fact that I was far from the sources of information which were necessary to treat the subject adequately. The paper which I read on the occasion of the lecture, entitled 'The Evolution of Religion Among American Negroes', presented in barest outlines the thesis of this book. It had been my hope, at the time, that when I returned to the United States I would be able to expand the original lecture on the basis of the materials which I had in my files. But it turned out that previously contracted writing obligations and teaching requirements delayed my expanding the lecture for publication. One compensating feature of the delay has been that it enabled me to give more reflection to the subject as well as to consult new sources of information. However, the basic thesis of the lecture has not been changed, namely, that the changes in the religious life of the Negro in the United States can be understood only in terms of the social organization and social disorganization of Negro life. The use of the term 'evolution' in the original title was perhaps unfortunate because it might have suggested that the lecture was concerned with stages in the development of religion among Negroes. This study, as now presented, is therefore concerned with the broad problem of the relation of religion to social structure or, more specifically, the role of religion in the social organization of Negro life in the United States.

There are a number of studies which have dealt with the Negro church and Negro religion in a general way, the most important among them being W. E. B. DuBois, *The Negro Church*; Carter G. Woodson, *The History of the Negro Church*; and

Benjamin E. Mays and Joseph W. Nicholson, *The Negro's Church*. To this number should be added Arthur H. Fauset's *Black Gods of the Metropolis*, which is the most valuable study of the new Negro cults in the city, and the descriptive material contained in the chapters dealing with religion in St. Clair Drake and Horace R. Cayton, *Black Metropolis*.

Grateful acknowledgement is due to the Council, Senate, and Faculty of Arts of the University of Liverpool for the invitation to give the Frazer Lecture and to Professor T. S. Simey both for the invitation and for his patience in waiting for the manuscript. A mere expression of gratitude is a small acknowledgement of my indebtedness to Mrs. Dorothy B. Porter of the Moorland Foundation Library, Howard University, whose wide knowledge of sources is indispensable to anyone working in the field of the Negro. Thanks are also due to Mrs. Louise C. Smith and Mrs. Willia P. Lewis for typing the manuscript under extremely difficult conditions. Finally, appreciation is due to my wife, whose father was a Baptist minister who built a school and established several churches, was a leader in fraternal organizations, and was once active in politics, for her intimate knowledge of the Negro church which was a part of her family heritage.

E. FRANKLIN FRAZIER

Washington, D.C.

THE NEGRO CHURCH
IN AMERICA

CHAPTER 1

The Religion of the Slaves

The Break with the African Background

IN studying any phase of the character and the development of the social and cultural life of the Negro in the United States, one must recognize from the beginning that because of the manner in which the Negroes were captured in Africa and enslaved, they were practically stripped of their social heritage.[1] Although the area in West Africa from which the majority of the slaves were drawn exhibits a high degree of cultural homogeneity, the capture of many of the slaves in inter-tribal wars and their selection for the slave markets tended to reduce to a minimum the possibility of the retention and the transmission of African culture. The slaves captured in the inter-tribal wars were generally males and those selected for the slave markets on the African coasts were the young and the most vigorous. This was all in accordance with the demands of the slave markets in the New World. One can get some notion of this selective process from the fact that it was not until 1840 that the number of females equalled the number of males in the slave population of the United States.[2] Young males, it will be readily agreed, are poor bearers of the cultural heritage of a people.

But the manner in which the slaves were held for the slave ships that transported them to the New World also had an important influence upon the transmission of the African social

1. This statement will appear to be in sharp disagreement with the position of Melville J. Herskovits who in his *The Myth of the Negro Past* (New York, 1924) undertakes to show that African survivals can be discovered in almost all phases of Negro life in the United States. However, in arranging the areas of Negro concentration in the New World on a scale according to the intensity of African survivals, he places the area of most intense survival in Suriname and says concerning the United States that it can be set off 'from the rest of the New World as a region where departure from African modes of life was greatest, and where such Africanisms as persisted were carried through in generalized form, almost never directly referable to a specific tribe or a definite area'. *Ibid.*, p. 122.

2. See Bureau of the Census, *Negroes in the United States, 1920–32*, p. 78.

heritage to the new environment. They were held in baracoons, an euphemistic term for concentration camps at the time, where the slaves without any regard for sex or family and tribal affiliations were kept until some slaver came along to buy a cargo for the markets of the New World. This period of de-humanization was followed by the 'middle passage', the voyage across the Atlantic Ocean to the slave markets of the West Indies and finally the indigo, tobacco, and cotton plantations of what was to become later the United States. During the 'middle passage', the Negroes were packed spoon-fashion in the slave ships where no regard was shown for sex or age differences, not to mention such matters as clan and tribal differences. In fact, no regard was shown for such elementary social, or shall I say human, considerations as family ties.

In the New World the process by which the Negro was stripped of his social heritage and thereby, in a sense, dehuman-ized was completed.[3] There was first the size of the plantation which had a significant influence upon the extent and nature of the contacts between the slaves and the whites. On the large sugar and cotton plantations in the Southern States there was, as in Brazil and the West Indies, little contact between whites and the Negro slaves. Under such conditions there was some opportunity for the slaves to undertake to re-establish their old ways. As a matter of fact, however, the majority of slaves in the United States were on small farms and small plantations. In some of the upland cotton regions of Alabama, Mississippi, Louisiana, and Arkansas the median number of slaves per hold-ing did not reach twenty; while in regions of general agriculture based mainly upon slave labour in Kentucky, Maryland, Missouri, North Carolina, South Carolina, and Tennessee the median number of slave holdings was even smaller.[4]

Then slaves freshly imported from Africa were usually 'broken in' to the plantation régime. According to the descrip-tions given by a traveller in Louisiana, the new slaves were only 'gradually accustomed to work. They are made to bathe often, to take long walks from time to time, and especially to dance;

3. See E. Franklin Frazier, *The Negro in the United States*, Revised (New York, 1957), Chapter I, concerning the manner in which the Negro was completely stripped of his African social heritage.

4. Lewis C. Gray, *History of Agriculture in the Southern United States to 1860* (New York, 1941), Vol. I, pp. 534–35.

they are distributed in small numbers among old slaves in order to dispose them better to acquire their habits.'[5] Apparently from all reports, these new slaves with their African ways were subjected to the disdain, if not hostility, of Negroes who had become accommodated to the plantation régime and had acquired the ways of their new environment.

Of what did accommodation to their new environment consist? It was necessary to acquire some knowledge of the language of whites for communication. Any attempt on the part of the slaves to preserve or use their native language was discouraged or prohibited. They were set to tasks in order to acquire the necessary skills for the production of cotton or sugar cane. On the small farms very often the slaves worked in the fields with their white owners. On the larger plantations they were under the strict discipline of the overseers who not only supervised their work but who also in the interest of security maintained a strict surveillance over all their activities. It was a general rule that there could be no assembly of five or more slaves without the presence of a white man. This applied especially to their gathering for religious purposes. Later we shall see how the slaves were soon introduced into the religious life of their white masters. All of this tended to bring about as completely as possible a loss of the Negro's African cultural heritage.

The Loss of Social Cohesion

It is evident, then, that the manner in which Negroes were captured and enslaved and inducted into the plantation régime tended to loosen all social bonds among them and to destroy the traditional basis of social cohesion. In addition, the organization of labour and the system of social control and discipline on the plantation both tended to prevent the development of social cohesion either on the basis of whatever remnants of African culture might have survived or on the basis of the Negroes' role in the plantation economy. Although the Negroes were organized in work gangs, labour lost its traditional African meaning as a co-operative undertaking with communal signifi-

5. 'Voyages . . . de la Louisiane', Vol. III, pp. 169–70, by C. C. Robin in Ulrich B. Phillips (ed.), *Plantation and Frontier: Documents: 1649–1863* (Cleveland, The A. H. Clark Co., 1909), p. 31.

cance. In fact, there was hardly a community among the slaves despite the fact that on the larger plantations there were slave quarters. These slave quarters were always under the surveillance of the overseer. On the smaller plantations which included, as we have seen, the majority of the plantations, the association between master and slave became the basis of a new type of social cohesion. However, this will be discussed in the next section.

Let us consider next a factor of equal if not greater importance in the plantation régime that tended to destroy all social cohesion among the slaves. I refer to the mobility of the slave population which resulted from the fact that the plantation in the Southern States was a commercial form of agriculture requiring the buying and selling of slaves. There has been much controversy about the slave-trade because of its dehumanizing nature. Curiously enough, southern apologists for slavery deny, on the one hand, that there was a domestic slave while, on the other hand, they insist that slave traders were despised and were regarded as outcasts in southern society.[6] There were defenders, however, of the system who frankly acknowledged that slave-trading was indispensable to the slave system. The Charleston *Mercury*, for example, stated that 'Slaves . . . are as much and as frequently articles of commerce as the sugar and molasses which they produce'.[7] This opinion has been confirmed by the study of the practice during slavery.[8] The slave-trade, we may conclude, was one of the important factors that tended towards the atomization and dehumanizing of the slaves.

The possibility of establishing some basis for social cohesion was further reduced because of the difficulty of communication among the slaves. If by chance slaves who spoke the same African language were thrown together, it was the policy on the part of the masters to separate them. In any case it was necessary for the operation of the plantation that the slaves should learn the language of their masters and communication among slaves themselves was generally carried on in English. In recent

6. See Ulrich B. Phillips, *American Negro Slavery* (New York, 1936). Chapter XI, where the author takes the position that slave-trading was uneconomical and that it was generally condemned.

7. Quoted in Frederic Bancroft, *Slave-Trading in the Old South* (Baltimore, 1939), p. 365.

8. See *ibid. passim.*

years a study has revealed that among the relatively isolated Negroes on the sea islands along the coast of South Carolina and Georgia, many African words have been preserved in the Negro dialect known as Gullah.[9] But the very social isolation of these Negroes is an indication of the exceptional situation in which some remnants of African languages were preserved in the American environment. It is important to note that, according to the author of this study, the use of African modes of English speech and African speech survivals were used only within the family group. This brings us to the most important aspect of the loss of social cohesion among the Negroes as the result of enslavement.

The enslavement of the Negro not only destroyed the traditional African system of kinship and other forms of organized social life but it made insecure and precarious the most elementary form of social life which tended to sprout anew, so to speak, on American soil—the family. There was, of course, no legal marriage and the relation of the husband and father to his wife and children was a temporary relationship dependent upon the will of the white masters and the exigencies of the plantation régime.[10] Although it was necessary to show some regard for the biological tie between slave mother and her offspring, even this relationship was not always respected by the masters. Nevertheless, under the most favourable conditions of slavery as, for example, among the privileged skilled artisans and the favoured house-servants, some stability in family relations and a feeling of solidarity among the members of the slave households did develop. This, in fact, represented the maximum social cohesion that was permitted to exist among the transplanted Negroes.

There have been some scholars who have claimed that social cohesion among the slaves was not destroyed to the extent to which it is presented here. For example, DuBois evidently thought that social cohesion among the slaves was not totally destroyed. For in one of his studies of Negro life he makes the assertion that the Negro church was 'the only social institution

9. See Lorenzo D. Turner, *Africanisms in the Gullah Dialect* (Chicago, 1949), p. 40.

10. See the author's *The Negro Family in the United States* (Chicago, 1939), Part I, concerning the Negro family during slavery.

among the Negroes which started in the African forest and survived slavery' and that 'under the leadership of the priest and medicine man' the church preserved the remnants of African tribal life.[11] From the available evidence, including what we know of the manner in which the slaves were Christianized and the character of their churches, it is impossible to establish any continuity between African religious practices and the Negro church in the United States. It is more likely that what occurred in America was similar to what Mercier has pointed out in regard to the Fon of Dahomey.[12] His studies showed that with the breaking up or destruction of the clan and kinship organization, the religious myths and cults lost their significance. In America the destruction of the clan and kinship organization was more devastating and the Negroes were plunged into an alien civilization in which whatever remained of their religious myths and cults had no meaning whatever.

The Christian Religion Provides a New Basis of Social Cohesion

It is our position that it was not what remained of African culture or African religious experience but the Christian religion that provided the new basis of social cohesion. It follows then that in order to understand the religion of the slaves, one must study the influence of Christianity in creating solidarity among a people who lacked social cohesion and a structured social life.

From the beginning of the importation of slaves into the colonies, Negroes received Christian baptism. The initial opposition to the christening of Negroes gradually disappeared when laws made it clear that slaves did not become free through the acceptance of the Christian faith and baptism.[13] Although slaves were regularly baptized and taken into the Anglican church during the seventeenth century, it was not until the opening of the eighteenth century that a systematic attempt was made on the part of the Church of England to Christianize Negroes in America. This missionary effort was carried out by

11. W. E. B. DuBois, *Some Efforts of the American Negroes for Their Own Betterment* (Atlanta, Ga., 1898).

12. P. Mercier, 'The Fon in Dahomey', in *African Worlds* (London, 1954), p. 234.

13. See Helen T. Catterall (ed.), *Judicial Cases Concerning American Slavery and the Negro* (Washington, D.C., 1926), Vol. I, p. 57. See also Lorenzo J. Greene, *The Negro in Colonial New England* (New York, 1942), Chapter X.

the Society for the Propagation of the Gospel in Foreign Parts which was chartered in England in 1701.[14] When the Indians in South Carolina proved to be so hostile to the first missionary sent out by the Society, he turned his attention to Negro and Indian slaves.

Unfortunately, we do not possess very detailed records on the religious behaviour of the Negroes who became converts to Christianity through the missionary efforts of the Society,[15] nor did the missionaries who worked under the auspices of the Moravians, Quakers, Presbyterians, and Catholics leave illuminating accounts of the response of the Negro slaves to their efforts. We do not know, for example, to what extent the converted slaves resumed their old 'heathen' ways or combined the new religious practices and beliefs with the old. In this connection it should be noted that the missionaries recognized the difficulty of converting the adult Africans and concentrated their efforts on the children.[16] However, there is no evidence that there was the type of syncretism or fusion of Christian beliefs and practices with African religious ideas and rituals such as one finds in the Candomblé in Brazil.[17] Despite the reported success in the conversion of Negroes, a study of the situation has revealed that only a small proportion of the slaves in the American colonies could be included among even nominal Christians.[18] In fact, the activities of the Anglican missionaries were directed to individuals whose isolation in the great body of slaves was increased.

As Woodson, the Negro historian, has so aptly called it, 'The Dawn of the New Day' in the religious development of Negroes occurred when the Methodists and Baptists began proselyting the blacks.[19] The proselyting activities on the part of the

14. C. F. Pascoe, *Two Hundred Years of the S.P.G.: An Historical Account of the Society for the Propagation of the Gospel in Foreign Parts* (London, 1901), Vol. I, pp. 1–7.

15. See *ibid.*, p. 16, concerning some of the activity of one missionary.

16. See 'The Bishop of London's Letter to the Masters and Mistresses in the English Plantations', quoted in Charles C. Jones, *The Religious Instruction of Negroes in the United States* (Savannah, 1842), p. 16.

17. See Arthur Ramos, *The Negro in Brazil* (Washington, D.C., 1939).

18. Marcus W. Jernegan, 'Slavery and Conversion in the American Colonies', *The American Historical Review*, Vol. XXI (April 1916), pp. 504–27.

19. Carter G. Woodson, *The History of the Negro Church*, 2nd edn. (Washington, D.C., 1921), Chapter II.

Methodists and Baptists, as well as the less extensive missionary work of the Presbyterians, were a phase of the Great Awakening which began in New England and spread to the West and South.[20] When the Methodists and Baptists began their revivals in the South, large numbers of Negroes were immediately attracted to this type of religious worship. However, it was not until after the American Revolution that large masses of the Negro population became converts and joined the Methodist and Baptist churches. During the closing years of the eighteenth century the religious revivals in Kentucky and Tennessee tended to re-enforce the forms of conversion which characterized the Methodist revivals and were used in some places by the Baptists and Presbyterians.[21]

Why did the Negro slaves respond so enthusiastically to the proselyting efforts of the Methodists and Baptists? From what has been pointed out concerning the manner in which the slaves were stripped of their cultural heritage, we may dismiss such speculations as the one that it was due to their African background.[22] We are on sounder ground when we note first that the Baptist and Methodist preachers, who lacked the education of the ministers of the Anglican church, appealed to the poor and the ignorant and the outcast. In the crowds that attended the revivals and camp meetings there were numbers of Negroes who found in the fiery message of salvation a hope and a prospect of escape from their earthly woes. Moreover, the emphasis which the preachers placed upon feeling as a sign of conversion found a ready response in the slaves who were repressed in so many ways. Then there were other factors in the situation that caused the slaves to respond to the forms of religious expression provided by the Baptists and Methodists. As we have indicated, the slaves who had been torn from their homeland and kinsmen and friends and whose cultural heritage was lost, were isolated and broken men, so to speak. In the

20. Joseph Tracy, *A History of the Great Awakening* (Boston, 1892), pp. 81–2.

21. See Catherine C. Cleveland, *The Great Revival in the West, 1797–1805* (Chicago, 1916), and Elizabeth K. Nottingham, *Methodism and the Frontier* (New York, 1941).

22. See, for example, the opinion of Herskovits, concerning the influence of African river-cults. 'Social History of the Negro', in Carl Murchison, *A Handbook of Social Psychology* (Worcester, 1935), pp. 256–7.

emotionalism of the camp meetings and revivals some social solidarity, even if temporary, was achieved, and they were drawn into a union with their fellow men. Later, common religious beliefs and practices and traditions tended to provide a new basis of social cohesion in an alien environment. We shall have more to say about this as we analyse further the development of religion among the slaves.

Not only did religion draw the Negroes into a union with their fellow-men, it tended to break down barriers that isolated them morally from their white masters. Where the plantation tended to become a social as well as an industrial institution, the Negro slaves participated in the religious life of their masters. It was a part of the discipline on many plantations to provide for the religious instruction of the slaves. The house servants often attended the family prayers. As a rule the galleries in the white churches were reserved for the Negro slaves.[23] The master, and more especially mistress, gave religious instruction to the slaves, and white ministers often preached to Negro congregations and supervised their activities. Thus, despite the vast gulf in the status that separated master and slave, participation in the same religious services drew the Negroes out of their moral isolation in the white man's world.

Christianity: A New Orientation Towards Existence

The uprooting of Negroes and the transportation of them to an alien land undoubtedly had a shattering effect upon their lives. In destroying their traditional culture and in breaking up their social organization, slavery deprived them of their accustomed orientation towards the world. Contrary to early misconceptions and still popularly held beliefs concerning the primitiveness of African religions, the peoples from which the slaves were drawn possessed developed systems of religious beliefs concerning their place in nature and in society.[24] In the crisis which they experienced the enslaved Negroes appealed to their ancestors and their gods. But their ancestors and their

23. See *Proceedings of the Meeting in Charleston, South Carolina, May 13–15, 1845 on the Religious Instruction of the Negroes* (Charleston, S.C., 1845).

24. See *African Worlds* with an 'Introduction' by Daryll Forde (London, 1954), which contains studies of the world-outlook and religious attitudes of a number of African peoples.

gods were unable to help them. Some slaves committed suicide during the 'middle passage' while others sought the same means of escape from bondage in the new environment.[25] The vast majority of the slaves submitted to their fate and in their confusion and bewilderment sought a meaning for their existence in the new white man's world.

The new orientation to the world was provided by Christianity as communicated to the slaves by their white masters. Naturally those elements among the slaves who worked and lived in close association with the whites were more influenced by Christian teachings and practices than the slaves who had few contacts with the whites. Those slaves who were largely isolated from the whites engaged in religious practices that undoubtedly included some African survivals. However, the whites were always on guard against African religious practices which could provide an opportunity for slave revolts, and they outlawed such practices. Moreover, there were efforts on the part of the whites to bring the slaves increasingly under the influence of the Christian religion. This was accomplished in part by acquainting the slaves with the Bible.

There were some misgivings and in some instances strong opposition to acquainting the Negro with the Bible. This fear of teaching the slaves the Bible was tied up with the laws against teaching slaves to read and write. But it was also feared that the slave would find in the Bible the implications of human equality which would incite the Negro to make efforts to free himself. Opposition to teaching the Negro the Bible declined as masters became convinced that sufficient justification for slavery could be found in the New Testament. In fact, some masters became convinced that some of the best slaves—that is, those amenable to control by their white masters—were those who read the Bible.[26]

Of course, the illiterate slaves could not gain a first-hand

25. It seems that slaves with certain tribal backgrounds were more addicted to suicide than others. Suicide was regarded by some slaves, it appears, as a means of returning to their homeland. See 'Practical Rules for the Management and Medical Treatment of Negro Slaves in the Sugar Colonies', by a Professional Planter (London, 1803), in Ulrich B. Phillips, *Documentary History of American Industrial Society: Plantation and Frontier Documents: 1649–1863* (Cleveland, 1909), Vol. II, pp. 128–9.

26. See Susan M. Fickling, *Slave-Conversion in South Carolina: 1830–1860* (University of South Carolina, 1924), p. 18.

knowledge of the Bible. But for an illiterate people it possessed great influence as a source of supernatural knowledge because it was a sacred book. Perhaps it is safe to say that among no other people has the Bible provided a better illustration of Frazer's statement in the preface of the second edition of his *Passages of the Bible* than among the Negroes of the United States. Especially is this true when he speaks of 'the pathetic associations with which the faith and piety of many generations have invested the familiar words' and that it strengthens man in 'the blind conviction, or the trembling hope that somewhere, beyond these earthly shadows, there is a world of light eternal, where obstinate questionings of the mind will be answered and the heart find rest'.[27]

By this statement we do not intend to give the impression that the Negroes completely assimilated the moral idealism of Christianity or even understood the language of the Bible. Selected parts of the Bible, such as the Lord's Prayer and the Ten Commandments, were used by the masters for the religious instruction of the slaves. In addition, stories from the Bible were told in simple language to the slaves. The slaves became familiar with the well-known Biblical characters and their role in the drama of salvation as it was presented to the Negro. Through the medium of the Negro preacher the stories in the Bible were dramatized for the Negro and many characters and incidents were interpreted in terms of the Negro's experiences.

The Bible was the means by which the Negroes acquired a new theology. As we have noted, the Negroes who were brought to the New World undoubtedly carried memories of their gods. These memories were lost or forgotten and there was a determined effort on the part of the whites to prevent any resurgence of African religion. It was from the Bible that the slaves learned of the god of the white man and of his ways with the world and with men. The slaves were taught that the God with whom they became acquainted in the Bible was the ruler of the universe and superior to all other gods. They were taught that the God of the Bible punished and rewarded black men as well as white men. Black men were expected to accept their lot in this world and if they were obedient and honest and truthful they would be rewarded in the world after death. In a book of

27. James G. Frazer, *Passages of the Bible* (London, 1932), pp. ix–x.

sermons and dialogues prepared by a minister of the Protestant Episcopal Church in Maryland in 1743 for use by masters and mistresses in their families, the slave in the dialogue says: 'God will reward me; and indeed I have good reason to be content and thankful; and I sometimes think more so than if I was free and ever so rich and great; for then I might be tempted to love and serve myself more than God. . . . But now I can't help knowing my duty. I am to serve God in that state in which he has placed me. I am to do what my master orders me.'[28]

In providing a theology, and thereby a new orientation towards the world and man, the Bible provided the Negro with the rich imagery which has characterized the sermons of Negro preachers and the sacred folk-songs of the Negro.

The Negro Adapts Christianity to his Experience in the New World

The Negro slave found in Christianity a theology and a new orientation towards the world at large and in doing so he adapted the Christian religion to his psychological and social needs. One of the best sources of information on the manner in which the Negro adapted Christianity to his peculiar psychological and social needs is to be found in that great body of sacred folk music known as the 'Negro Spirituals'. In recent years there have been some efforts on the part of Negro intellectuals, encouraged sometimes by white radicals, to invest most of the Spirituals with a revolutionary meaning or to claim that they represented disguised plans for escape from slavery.[29] It is our position that the sacred folk-songs or Spirituals were essentially religious in sentiment and, as we shall see, otherworldly in outlook. We are aware that since the Spirituals are folk-songs they underwent changes which make it impossible to know what they were originally. Moreover, we are not unaware of the interpretations which often reflect the biases of whites. We recognize too that some of the folk-songs were undoubtedly composed for special occasions and, therefore, cannot be understood completely outside the framework of a particular time and place. Nevertheless, the sacred folk-songs

28. Rev. Thomas S. Bacon, *Sermons Addressed to Masters and Servants.* Published *in the Year 1743* (Winchester, Va., *circa* 1813), pp. 142–3.
29. See Miles M. Fisher, *Negro Slave Songs in the United States* (Ithaca, 1953), and John Lovell, 'The Social Implications of the Negro Spiritual', *Journal of Negro Education* (October, 1939).

express the awe and wonder of the Negro in regard to life and death and his emotional reactions to the complexity of his existence and his desire to escape from the uncertainties and frustrations of this world.

On the Sea Islands off the coast of South Carolina and Georgia where the slaves were most isolated from whites, some of the Spirituals reveal some continuity with their African background. This continuity is to be found especially in what has been called the Afro-American shout songs.[30] These shout songs are so named because they were sung and are still sung while the Negro worshippers are engaged in what might be called a holy dance. This may be regarded as an example of the most primitive and elemental expression of religion among American Negroes. Moreover, it provides an excellent illustration of Marett's contention that primitive man 'does not preach his religion, but dances it instead'.[31] Although the shout songs most likely reveal a connection with the African background, they were addressed to the 'Good Lord', or the white man's god. The influence of Christian ideology is revealed in other ways. These songs contain the idea of heaven and a judgment day when Gabriel will blow his trumpet.

In fact, in most of the Spirituals which have been gathered from all areas in the South, Christian ideology or theology is evident in practically all of them. The Christian theology is revealed in the Negro's conception of the world. His conception of the world is a world ruled by the Providence of an almighty God.[32] According to the words of one Spiritual:

> My God is a rock in a weary land,
> My God is a rock in a weary land,
> Shelter in time of storm.

From the standpoint of his earthly condition, the Negro was constantly concerned with death. In a recent lecture dealing

---

30. Lydia Parrish, *Slave Songs of the Georgia Sea Islands* (New York, 1942), pp. 54–92.

31. R. R. Marett, *The Threshold of Religion* (London, 1914), p. 175.

32. It is of interest to note in passing that whereas the idea of Providence is conspicuous in the religion of the American Negro, the idea of a Fate is apparently absent. In a recent study both ideas of Providence and Fate are to be found in the religious conceptions of West African Negroes. See Meyer Fortes, *Œdipus and Job in West African Religion* (Cambridge, 1959).

with the Spirituals, a distinguished Negro minister has pointed
out that for the slave death was an ever-present and compelling
fact 'because of the cheapness with which his life was regarded.
The slave was a tool, a thing, a utility, a commodity, but he
was not a person. He was faced constantly with the imminent
threat of death, of which the terrible overseer was the symbol;
and the awareness that he (the slave) was only chattel property,
the dramatization.'[33]

One only needs to recall the words of many of the Spirituals
to realize how important death was to the slaves and later to the
emancipated Negro. Their concern with death is shown in the
following words of a Spiritual[34] in which the worshippers sing:

> Come down, come down, my Lord,
> An' take me up to wear de crown.

And let us note that:

> My Lord's writin' all de time
> He sees all you do, hears all you say.

Death was not only always at hand, but it was also a terrible
experience because God holds one accountable for the way in
which one has behaved in this world.

> Death is gwinter lay his cold icy hands on me, Lord.
> Death is gwinter lay his cold icy hands on me,
> One mornin' I was walkin' along
> I heard a voice and saw no man;
> Said go in peace and sin no more,
> Yo' sins fo'given an' yo' soul set free.
> One of dese mornin's it won't be long,
> Yo'll look fo' me an' I'll be gone.[35]

The concern with death is connected with the predominantly
other-worldly outlook in the Negro's religion. In many of the
Spirituals death appears as a means of escape from the woes and

33. Howard Thurman, *The Negro Spiritual Speaks of Life and Death* (New
York, 1947), pp. 13–14.
34. James W. Johnson (ed.), *The Book of American Negro Spirituals*
(New York, 1937), pp. 123–4.
35. James W. Johnson, *The Second Book of American Negro Spirituals* (New
York, 1933), pp. 93–4.

weariness of this world. The words of an often sung Spiritual say that:

By and by, I'm goin' to lay down this heavy load.
By and by, by and by, I'm goin' to lay down this heavy load.[36]

Then when those who are 'saved' reach heaven, the words of another Spiritual read:

> I've got a robe, you've got a robe,
> All God's children got a robe,
> When I get to heaven goin' to put on my robe
> Goin' to shout all over God's heaven.[37]

For a people who had been separated from kinsmen and friends, it was inevitable that the ties of kinship formed in the New World should be the most valued form of human association. This was especially true in respect to the relationship between the mother and her children since, generally, no recognition was accorded the relationship between spouses and the father and his children. The words of a Spiritual tell of relatives in heaven:

> I've got a mother in de heaven,
>   Outshines de sun,
> I've got a father in de heaven,
>   Outshines de sun,
> I've got a sister in de heaven,
>   Outshines de sun,
> When we get to heaven, we will
>   Outshine de sun,
>   Way beyond de moon.[38]

As we have shown, the Negro slaves were lonely men. It was often in their loneliness that religion was a solace in that they could escape from their loneliness by communicating with God. The slaves would speak of walking and talking with God. They often became converted and found salvation when God spoke to them and told them that they were free of sin. Nevertheless, the slave, without secure family ties, was aware of his

36. R. Nathaniel Dett, *Religious Folk-Songs of the Negro* (Hampton, Va., 1927), p. 124.
37. *Ibid.*, p. 126.
38. *Ibid.*, p. 123.

loneliness in this world. In response to this feeling of loneliness
the slave might sing:

> Sometimes I feel like a motherless child,
> Sometimes I feel like a motherless child,
> A long ways from home.[39]

Or, perhaps, the religious implications of his loneliness were
expressed in the words of another Spiritual.

An' I couldn't hear nobody pray, O Lord,
O, way down yonder by myself and I couldn't hear nobody
pray,
Wid my burden, I couldn't hear nobody pray.[40]

More often, however, the religion of the Negro was expressed
in the Spirituals showing faith and fellowship with his fellow
slaves.

> I'm gwine to jine de great 'sociation,
> I'm gwine to jine de great 'sociation.
> Den my little soul's gwine to shine.

The great 'sociation was, at least as its earthly manifestations
were concerned, the 'invisible institution' of the Negro church.

The 'Invisible Institution' Comes into Existence

It is no exaggeration to say that the 'invisible institution' of
the Negro church took root among the enslaved blacks. The
key to an understanding of the 'invisible institution' may be
found in the typical remark of an ex-slave who wrote:

Our preachers were usually plantation folks just like the rest of us.
Some man who had a little education and had been taught something about the Bible would be our preacher. The coloured folks
had their code of religion, not nearly so complicated as the white
man's religion, but more closely observed. . . . When we had our
meetings of this kind, we held them in our own way and were not
interfered with by the white folks'.[41]

The observation of a Swedish visitor to the New World sheds

---

39. Johnson, *The Second Book of American Negro Spirituals*, p. 30.
40. Johnson, *The Book of American Negro Spirituals*, pp. 89–90.
41. Robert Anderson, *From Slavery to Affluence: Memories of Robert Anderson,
Ex-Slave* (Hemingford, Nebr., 1927), pp. 22–3.

more light upon the manner in which the 'invisible institution' of the Negro Church was accomplished. Concerning a visit near Charleston in 1851, she wrote:

in the village itself everything was still and quiet. A few Negro men and women were standing about, and they looked kind and well to do. I heard in one house a sound as of prayer and zealous exhortation. I entered, and saw the assemblage of Negroes, principally women, who were much edified and affected in listening to a Negro who was preaching to them with great fervour and great gesticulation, thumping on the table with his clenched fists. The sermon and substance of his sermon was this: 'Let us do as Christ has commanded us; let us love one another. Then he will come to us on our sickbeds, on our deathbeds, and he will make us free, and we shall come to him and sit with him in glory.'[42]

Since all forms of organized social effort were forbidden among the slaves and in the absence of an established priesthood, the Negro preacher played the important role in the 'invisible institution' of the church among the slaves. The Negro preacher was 'called' to his office and through his personal qualities achieved a position of dominance. The 'call' was supposed to have come through some religious experience which indicated that God had chosen him as a spiritual leader. According to Frederick Douglass, the abolitionist orator who escaped from slavery, the preacher was one of the slave notabilities.[43] The preacher to whom Douglass refers seems to have achieved his authority because of personal qualities. This authority was given greater weight when the slave who had been called to preach was licensed by the Methodist or Baptist Church.

One qualification which the Negro preacher among the slaves needed to possess was some knowledge of the Bible. However imperfect or distorted his knowledge of the Bible might be, the fact that he was acquainted with the source of sacred knowledge, which was in a sense the exclusive possession of his white masters, gave him prestige in matters concerning the supernatural and religious among his fellow slaves. His knowledge of the sacred scriptures had to be combined with an ability to speak and communicate his special knowledge to the slaves. As

42. Fredrika Bremer, *Homes in the New World*, translated by Mary Howitt (New York, 1853), Vol. I, pp. 289-90.

43. Frederick Douglass, *Life and Times of Frederick Douglass* (Chicago, 1882), p. 31.

one white minister pointed out, the religious instruction of the slaves required preaching rather than instruction in the Christian faith. Preaching meant dramatizing the stories of the Bible and the way of God to man. These slave preachers were noted for the imagery of their sermons. One slave preacher, John Jasper, achieved distinction, according to his biographer, because of his lofty dignity which was combined with his fiery and thrilling oratory despite his 'tempestuous and ungrammatical eloquence'.[44]

Another qualification which the slave preacher must possess was the ability to sing. From the beginning of religious expression among the slaves which was characterized by the 'shout songs', preaching on the part of the leader was important. This preaching consisted of singing sacred songs which have come to be known as the Spirituals. The singing of these preachers and for that matter preachers among the Negro masses later has been a sort of 'moaning'.[45] Usually, the singing of the Spirituals has accompanied the 'shouting' or holy dancing which has characterized this ecstatic form of religious worship among Negroes.

The Negro preacher among the slaves was more than a leader in these ephemeral gatherings whose members were held together by the emotional contagion which Marett has called the 'mobish' character of primitive religions.[46] Because of the local autonomy in Baptist churches in contrast to the centralized hierarchy of the Methodist church, the Negro preacher was free to exercise his gifts and to direct his followers. This also accounts in part at least for the larger number of slaves who were attracted to the Baptists. The leadership of the preacher was recognized by his 'congregation' and as far as the white masters were willing to concede to him this role among the slaves. Although the masters were unwilling to tolerate any form of organized activities among the slaves, different members

44. William E. Hatcher, *John Jasper, the Unmatched Negro Philosopher and Preacher* (New York, 1908).

45. Cf. Fisher, *op. cit.*, p. 187.

46. Marett, *op. cit.*, p. 175. An important differentiation may be made between the ecstatic religious behaviour of the crowd that 'dances' and the crowd which 'acts' and thus becomes a mob. See Robert E. Park and Ernest W. Burgess, *Introduction to the Science of Sociology* (Chicago, 1924), pp. 870 ff.

of the 'congregations' played various roles according to their talents as singers or according to their ability to influence other slaves to get converted or attend religious services.

The recognition which the whites accorded to the Negro 'congregations' was accorded them as segments of the white organizations. White control of these segments was never completely relaxed. Therefore, there was always some tension because the slaves preferred their own preachers and wanted to conduct their religious services according to their own mode of worshipping. This tension was always sharpened by the fact that there were free Negroes in the churches which were established in connection with the white church organizations. The tension was never resolved and the Negro church never emerged as an independent institution except under the Negroes who were free before the Civil War.

CHAPTER 2

The Institutional Church of the Free Negroes

Negroes who were Free before the Civil War

THE twenty Negroes who were sold to the Virginia settlers by a Dutch man-of-war in 1619 were not slaves since there was no precedent in English law for slavery. These Negroes and those imported later were 'absorbed in a growing system (servitude based upon English apprenticeship and vagrancy laws) which spread to all the colonies and for nearly a century furnished the chief supply of colonial labour'.[1] Little is known of what became of the first twenty Negroes who were introduced into the Virginia colony. However, there is a record of the baptism of a child of one couple among them. This is significant because at the time, according to the law of England by which the colony was governed, 'a slave who had been christened or baptized became "infranchised" '.[2] It appears that the original twenty Negroes were freed after seven years of indentured labour and that at least one among them, an Anthony Johnson, acquired considerable land after becoming free. As the enslavement of Negroes developed in practice and was confirmed by law, during the seventeenth century, Maryland as well as Virginia passed laws to the effect that Christian baptism did not confer freedom upon the slaves.

Nevertheless, the free Negro population in the colonies and later in the United States continued to increase until the outbreak of the Civil War. The increase in the free Negro population came from five sources: (1) children born of free coloured persons; (2) mulatto children born of coloured mothers; (3) mulatto children born of white servants or free women; (4) children of free Negro and Indian parentage; and (5) slaves who were set free.[3] It is difficult to estimate the proportion of

1. James C. Ballagh, *A History of Slavery in Virginia* (Baltimore, 1902), p. 32.
2. Helen T. Catterall (ed.), *Judicial Cases Concerning American Slavery and the Negro* (Washington, D.C., 1926), Vol. I, p. 55.
3. John H. Russell, *The Free Negro in Virginia: 1619–1865* (Baltimore, 1913), pp. 40–1.

the increase in the number of free Negroes attributable to each source. The growth in numbers resulting from natural increase continued until the Civil War. On the other hand, the accessions to the free Negro population through the unions of free and servant white women and free coloured women and white men were kept at a minimum because of the drastic laws against such unions.[4] Although there was constant intermixture of Negroes and Indians in areas reserved for Indians as well as outside these areas, there is no way of knowing to what extent this intermixture contributed to the growth of the free Negro population.

It appears that the manumission or the freeing of slaves was the main source through which the free Negro population increased. This was accomplished both by public and private action. Occasionally, public manumission came as a reward for some meritorious public service such as revealing a Negro conspiracy. A Pierre Chastang of Mobile, Alabama, was bought and freed by popular subscription in recognition of his services in the War of 1812 and in the yellow fever epidemic in 1819.[5] It is probable that some of the fevour in emancipating the slaves was due to the philosophy of the Revolution. This was the case in the North, at least, where slavery had no real economic base and was dying out. In the Southern States, Maryland and Virginia, there were legal restrictions upon private emancipation which was the means by which masters sometimes relieved themselves of slaves who could no longer be worked for profit.

The Negroes who were free before the Civil War were concentrated in the areas where the plantation system of agriculture either had not taken root or had died out. They were to be found chiefly in the tide-water region of Virginia and Maryland and the Piedmont region of North Carolina. Moreover, there were settlements of free Negroes in the North and in the isolated communities of Negroes mixed with Indians. But the majority of free Negroes were concentrated in the cities both in the North and in the South. It was in the urban areas of the South that the free Negroes were able to

4. See references in footnote 2, p. 59, in the author's *The Negro in the United States*.
5. Ulrich B. Phillips, *American Negro Slavery* (New York, 1936), p. 428.

achieve a secure position in the economic organization. On the other hand, in the cities of the North, the free Negroes were confronted with the competition of European immigrants and had a difficult time in surviving. In the North the free Negroes could acquire some education openly while in the South they had to secure education surreptitiously and through their own efforts. Since many free Negroes acquired their freedom as the result of being children of free coloured women and white men or slave women and white men who emancipated their coloured offspring, nearly two-fifths of the free Negroes were mulattoes or of mixed ancestry. In the cities of the South, especially in Charleston, South Carolina, and in New Orleans, the communities of free mulattoes became almost an intermediate caste between the whites and the slaves. They acquired considerable wealth, including slaves; they maintained conventional standards of sex and family life; they were cultivated people who often sent their children to Europe for education and in order to escape racial prejudice.

Among the free Negroes in both the North and the South, there developed an organized community life. Most of their efforts were concerned with mutual aid societies and co-operation for economic welfare. These organizations, including efforts to acquire an education, were generally tied up with their churches which comprised a large part of their wealth.[6] Their church organizations had come into existence as the result of the proselyting activities on the part of whites but had become important as the result of the efforts of the free Negroes themselves.

Relation of Free Negroes and Whites in the Churches

The relations of free Negroes and whites in the churches were determined largely by the slave status of the majority of the Negro population. Although the Anglican Church, as we have seen, carried on missionary activities among the slaves, they were not interested in changing the status of Negro slaves. It was the Quakers who in accepting both Negro slaves and free men on a basis of equality became the enemies of the system of slavery. As early as the seventeenth century the Quakers

6. See Carter G. Woodson, 'The Negroes of Cincinnati Prior to the Civil War', *The Journal of Negro History*, Vol. I (January 1916), pp. 1–22.

advocated the religious training of the slaves as a preparation for freedom. Many of the Quakers freed their slaves and helped to remove legal restrictions against the private manumission of slaves. The relation of the free Negroes to the whites in the churches did not become a real issue until the Negroes were evangelized by the Methodists and Baptists.

Among the early Baptist and Methodist missionaries, there were many who preached the liberation of the slave as a part of their creed. The Methodists required their travelling missionaries to set slaves free on the ground that slavery was contrary to the laws of God, man, and nature.[7] In 1784 the Methodist conference took steps towards the abolition of slavery, declaring that slavery was opposed to the laws of God and contrary to the principles of the American Revolution. However, the Baptists were winning more Negroes in their local meetings by their open attack on slavery. Gradually, both the Methodists and the Baptists receded from their position in face of the general opposition to their stand on the question of slavery.

The relation of the free Negroes to the white Christian churches may be seen first in the activities of the early Negro preachers and their relations with white congregations. This was natural since, as we have seen, the Negro preacher, slave as well as free, occupied a dominant position in the religious activities of Negroes. The traditional African priesthood had disappeared and a church organization only grew up gradually among the Negroes. The oldest or next to the oldest Negro Baptist church to be established in the United States was due to the efforts of George Liele, a slave born in Virginia about 1750 and taken by his master to Georgia before the Revolutionary War.[8] As the result of accompanying his master, who was a deacon, to church he was converted and baptized. Because of his 'unusual ministerial gifts', he was permitted to preach on the plantations and later he was liberated by his master to carry on his work as a minister. His master was killed in the Revolutionary War and when the heirs raised some question about his free status, Liele followed the British when

7. Woodson, *The History of the Negro Church*, p. 27.
8. See Woodson, *The History of the Negro Church*, Chapter III, 'Pioneer Negro Preachers'.

they evacuated Savannah. Before leaving Savannah, he baptized Andrew Bryan and some other Negroes who became the founders of the African Baptist Church in Savannah.

Andrew Bryan was born a slave in South Carolina and was brought by his master to Savannah. He began with public exhortations and prayer meetings and was soon preaching to congregations of white and black people in Savannah. Bryan was permitted by his master and other whites to erect a church. But considerable opposition developed because it was feared that despite the 'salutary' effect of his preaching, the religious gatherings would lead to a slave uprising. Bryan and his brother suffered considerable persecution including whippings and torture. His master came to his defence and he was permitted to conduct his services in a barn. Through the assistance of influential friends he was able to collect funds in order to purchase a lot upon which he built a church. When his master died, the heirs of the estate gave him an opportunity to purchase his freedom. However, the church remained under the control of the heirs of his master's estate and the worship of the communicants continued to be supervised by whites. As the membership increased a number of congregations split and new churches were founded. When Bryan died in 1812, he was the acknowledged and respected leader of the religious life of Negroes in Georgia.

The pioneering work of Negro Baptist preachers was more successful in those areas of the South where the interests of the ruling whites were not so deeply rooted in the plantation system. This was especially true in the cities of Virginia where a number of Baptist churches were established in the last decade of the eighteenth century and during the early years of the nineteenth century. Moreover, there were outstanding Negro preachers who had embraced the Methodist faith and were pioneers in establishing congregations among their fellow slaves and freedmen. One famous Negro preacher, known as Black Harry and described as 'small, very black, keen-eyed, possessing great volubility of tongue', accompanied Asbury and was declared by Dr. Benjamin Rush to be the greatest orator in America.[9] Black Harry and other Negro Methodist preachers, as many Negro Baptist preachers had done, preached

9. See *ibid.*, pp. 56–7.

to white as well as Negro congregations. But there was always some question concerning the propriety of Negroes preaching to whites. There was even opposition to whites and Negroes worshipping together. What happened in the case of a Negro preacher in Northampton, Virginia, towards the end of the eighteenth century may be taken as typical. The white Baptist association stated that 'whereas the black brethren in the church seemed anxious for a vote in the conference that it would be best to consider the black people as a wing of the body',[10] and that Josiah Bishop, a famous Negro preacher who had been pastor of the mixed congregation, be assigned pastor of the black congregation. The Negro communicants did not press their desire to vote and continued in their subordinate position. Josiah Bishop went to Baltimore and later to New York to become pastor of the Abyssinian Baptist Church.

Conflict Over the Question of Status

It is apparent then that in the early development of the Negro church on an institutional basis there was the question of the status of the Negro preachers and Negro communicants in relation to the white church organizations. In the South where slavery was the normal condition of the Negro or as the Supreme Court of Mississippi stated that the laws of the State 'presume a Negro *prima facie* to be a slave', it was to be expected that the question of the status of the Negro in the churches should be insistent. In fact, the schism which was created in the various national church organizations over the question of slavery involved the status of the Negro in the Christian churches. After many attempts to reconcile the viewpoint of the southern sections of these church organizations which sought justification of slavery in the Scriptures with that of northern elements who refused to justify slavery on Christian grounds, the Methodists, Baptists, and Presbyterians split and set up separate organizations. In the South the Negroes continued to join the Methodist and Baptist churches in large numbers and to worship in the segregated sections of the churches of their masters. In many places, the situation in Charleston, South Carolina, being typical, the Presbyterians and Episcopalians built separate churches for their Negro members. As the

10. Quoted in *ibid.*, p. 55.

Negro membership increased, the Baptists and Methodists too provided their Negro members with separate churches. In these separate church organizations the Negroes tended to conduct their services according to their own mode of religious expression though under white supervision. But there was always an urge to achieve a certain degree of autonomy on the part of Negro congregations.

The question of status was not confined to the South.[11] In the North as in the South a number of Negro preachers had acquired some distinction and had preached to predominantly white congregations. Among these was Lemuel Haynes, the illegitimate child of a Negro and a white woman who was born in Connecticut in 1753. He took the name of a white benefactor who took him in his home when he was abandoned by his mother. Haynes grew to manhood in Massachusetts after having been bound out as a child of five months. It was in the home of the man to whom he was bound out that he first read the Bible and conducted the family prayers. He was licensed to preach in the Congregational Church and served in a number of churches in New England.[12]

The most famous of the Negro preachers in the North was, in a sense, Richard Allen because of the role which he played in the organization of an independent Negro church organization.[13] Allen was born a slave in Philadelphia but was sold to a planter who took him to Delaware. He early came under the influence of Methodist preachers and was converted in 1777. He was allowed to conduct prayers and preach in the house of his master who became converted. In the same year, he and his brother were permitted to purchase their freedom from their master, who had become convinced that slavery was wrong, for $2,000 in depreciated Continental currency.[14]

After becoming free, Allen engaged in odd jobs but remained intensely religious and became a preacher in 1780. In recognition of his talents as a preacher he was allowed to travel with

11. See, for example, 'The Negro Pew' Being an Inquiry Concerning the Propriety of Distinctions in the House of God on Account of Color (Boston, 1837).

12. Woodson, op. cit., pp. 61–5.

13. Ibid., pp. 73 ff.

14. Richard Allen, The Life, Experience and Gospel Labors of Rt. Rev. Richard Allen (Philadelphia, n.d.), p. 12. See also Charles H. Wesley, Richard Allen, Apostle of Freedom (Washington, D.C., 1935), pp. 15–17.

white ministers and given assignments by Bishop Asbury. When he went to Philadelphia in 1786 he was invited to preach in the St. George Methodist Episcopal Church. When Allen observed in Philadelphia the need of the Negroes for religious leadership and an organization, he proposed that a separate church be established for Negroes. His proposal was opposed both by whites and Negroes. However, when the number of Negroes attending St. George Methodist Episcopal Church increased, Negroes were removed from the seats around the wall and ordered to sit in the gallery. Mistaking the section of the gallery which they were to occupy, Allen, Absalom Jones, and another member were almost dragged from their knees as they prayed.[15] They left the church and together with other Negro members founded the Free African Society.

The Free Negroes Establish their own Churches

After Richard Allen and Absalom Jones organized the Free African Society, they differed as to whether Negroes should model their church organization after the Methodist or after the Protestant Episcopal Church. Allen was of the opinion that the Methodist form of worship was more suited to the religious needs and form of worship to which the Negroes had become accustomed. As a consequence of this difference between Jones and Allen, Jones organized the African Protestant Episcopal Church of St. Thomas but the majority of the Negroes who had seceded from the white church followed Allen. Allen organized the Bethel Church for which an old building was purchased and dedicated in 1794. Bishop Asbury ordained Allen a deacon and later he became an elder. The movement begun by Allen under the name of African societies spread to other cities where so-called African Methodist Episcopal Churches were set up. There was some co-operation among the leaders of the separate church organizations in the various cities. As a result, the representatives of these churches met in Philadelphia in 1816 and established the African Methodist Episcopal Church. At this meeting Allen was elected bishop and a book of discipline was adopted which embodied the same articles of religion and rules as the Wesleyans.[16]

15. See Wesley, *op. cit.*, pp. 52–3.
16. Woodson, pp. 75–7.

The secession of Negroes from the white Methodist church in Philadelphia was followed by secessions in New York City. Peter Williams, Sr., whose son became the first Negro to be ordained as a priest in the Protestant Episcopal Church, was himself a sexton for a number of years in the John Street Methodist Church. He was distinguished for his piety and faithfulness among the white communicants. However, being influenced by the general movement among Negroes to establish their own churches, he joined with other Negroes in organizing the Zion Church out of which developed the African Methodist Episcopal Zion Church. During this period independent Baptist churches were being established by Negroes in the Southern States, Maryland, Virginia, Georgia, and Kentucky, and in northern cities, Boston, New York City, and Philadelphia. It was only much later that these Negro Baptist churches were brought together in a national convention. On a much smaller scale Negroes organized Protestant Episcopal, Presbyterian, and Congregational churches. As the result of Emancipation still another Negro Methodist organization came into existence. When the split occurred in the Methodist Church in 1844 over the question of slavery, the Negroes continued, as we have seen, to join and worship in the churches of their masters while in the North there were Negro congregations which continued to be connected with the Methodist Episcopal Church. After the Civil War, the small Negro membership which remained in the Methodist Episcopal Church South was permitted to organize a separate body. Thus, there came into existence the Colored Methodist Episcopal Church in Jackson, Tennessee, in 1870. In these various Methodist and Baptist church organizations, nearly a half of the Negroes have remained, on the whole, to the present day.

CHAPTER 3

The Negro Church: A Nation Within a Nation

The 'Invisible Institution' Merges with the Institutional Church

THE Civil War and Emancipation destroyed whatever stability and order that had developed among Negroes under the slave régime. An educated mulatto minister of the African Methodist Episcopal Church who went from the North to the South following Emancipation wrote:

The whole section (in the neighbourhood of Charleston, South Carolina) with its hundreds of thousands of men, women and children just broken forth from slavery, was, so far as these were concerned, dying under an almost physical and moral interdict. There was no one to baptize their children, to perform marriage, or to bury the dead. A ministry had to be created at once—created out of the material at hand.[1]

The 'material at hand' was, of course, those Negroes among the slaves who had been 'called to preach'. In answer to the criticism that neither men nor money were available for creating a ministry, the minister just quoted wrote that 'God could call the men; and that the A.M.E. Church had the authority to commission them when thus called'. This represented the fusion of the 'invisible institution' of the Negro church which had taken root among the slaves and the institutional church which had grown up among the Negroes who were free before the Civil War.

The most obvious result of the merging of the 'invisible institution' of the church which had grown up among the slaves with the institutional church of the Negroes who were free before the Civil War was the rapid growth in the size of the Negro church organization. But there was a much more important result of this merger which is of primary concern to our study. The merger resulted in the structuring or organization of Negro life to an extent that had not existed. This

1. Theophilus G. Steward, *Fifty Years in the Gospel Ministry* (Philadelphia, 1915), p. 33.

becomes clear when we recall that organized social life among the transplanted Negroes had been destroyed by slavery. The traditional African clan and family had been destroyed and in the environment of the New World the development of a structured family life was always nullified by the exigencies of the plantation system. Any efforts towards organization in their religious life was prevented because of the fear of the whites of slave insurrections. Even any spontaneous efforts towards mutual aid on an organized basis was prevented for the same reasons. There was, to be sure, some social differentiation among the slaves based upon the different roles which they played in the plantation economy. But this did not result in the structuring of the social life among the slaves themselves. Among the slaves themselves one may note the germs of stratification based upon their different roles in the plantation, but no system of stratification ever came into existence that became the basis of an organized social existence.

This was all changed when the Negro became free and it is our purpose here to show how an organized religious life became the chief means by which a structured or organized social life came into existence among the Negro masses. The process by which the 'invisible institution' of the slaves merged with the institutional churches built by the free Negroes had to overcome many difficulties. These difficulties arose chiefly from the fact that there were among the free Negroes many mulattoes and that they, as well as the unmixed Negroes, represented a higher degree of assimilation of white or European culture. This was often reflected in the difference in the character of the religious services of those with a background of freedom and those who were just released from slavery. In fact, in the social stratification of the Negro population after Emancipation, a free and mulatto ancestry became the basis of important social distinctions.[2] It should be pointed out, however, that these cultural and social distinctions were reflected in the denominational affiliation of Negroes. The Negro masses were concentrated in the Methodist and Baptist churches which provided for a more emotional and ecstatic form of worship than the Protestant Episcopal, Presbyterian, and Congrega-

2. See E. Franklin Frazier, *The Negro Family in the United States* (Chicago, 1939), Chapter XIX, 'Old Families and New Classes'.

tional churches. But even in the Methodist and Baptist denominations there were separate church organizations based upon distinctions of colour and what were considered standards of civilized behaviour. In the Methodist and Baptist churches in which the vast majority of Negroes were communicants, it was impractical to organize separate churches which would be congenial to the way of life of the small Negro *élite*. Nevertheless, some of the educated leaders were not in sympathy with the more primitive religious behaviour of the masses. The attitude of educated leaders of even Methodist and Baptist churches was expressed by a Bishop in the African Methodist Episcopal Church even before Emancipation. He opposed the singing of the Spirituals which he described as 'corn field ditties' and songs of 'fist and heel worshippers' and said that the ministry of the A.M.E. Church must drive out such 'heathenish mode of worship' or 'drive out all intelligence and refinement'.[3]

Despite the difficulties, the integration of the 'invisible institution' which had emerged among the slaves into the Negro church organization established by the free Negroes was achieved. This provided an organization and structuring of Negro life which has persisted until the present time. We shall begin by considering the relation of the organization of the religious life of the Negro to building up of social control.

The Church as an Agency of Social Control

In dealing with the Negro church as an agency of control we shall focus attention upon the relation of the church to the Negro family and sex life during the years following Emancipation. In order to understand the important role of the Negro church, it is necessary to have a clear conception of the situation which confronted organized religion. Under slavery the Negro family was essentially an amorphous group gathered around the mother or some female on the plantation. The father was a visitor to the household without any legal or recognized status in family relations. He might disappear as the result of the sale of slaves or because of a whimsical change of his own feelings or affection. Among certain favoured elements on the plantation, house slaves and skilled artisans, the family might achieve greater stability and the father and husband might

3. Quoted in Fisher, *Negro Slave Songs in the United States*, pp. 189–90.

develop a more permanent interest in his family. Whatever might be the circumstances of the Negro family under the slave régime, family and sex relations were constantly under the supervision of the whites.

The removal of the authority of masters as the result of the Civil War and Emancipation caused promiscuous sex relations to become widespread and permitted the constant changing of spouses. The daughter of a planter family who has idealized the slave régime nevertheless tells a story which illustrates the disorder. 'Mammy Maria', she wrote, 'came out in the new country as "Miss Dabney", and attracted, as she informed her "white children", as much admiration as any of the young girls, and had offers of marriage too. But she meant to enjoy her liberty, she said, and should not think of marrying any of them.'[4] Some of the confusion in marital relations was due, of course, to the separation of husbands and wives during slavery and the social disorganization that resulted from Emancipation.

The problem of monogamous and stable family life was one of the most vexing problems that confronted northern white missionaries who undertook to improve the morals of the newly liberated blacks. These missionaries undertook to persuade the freedmen to legalize and formalize their marriages. There was resistance on the part of many of the slaves since legal marriage was not in their *mores*. Sometimes missionaries even attempted to use force in order that the freedmen legalize their sexual unions. There were, of course, many cases in which the marriage ceremony was a confirmation of a union that was based upon conjugal sentiment established over a long period of association. Marriage and an institutional family life could not be imposed by white missionaries. Marriage and the family could acquire an institutional character only as the result of the operation of economic and social forces within the Negro communities.

A large proportion of the Negro families among the freedmen continued after Emancipation to be dependent upon the Negro mother as they had been during slavery. But the new economic conditions which resulted from Emancipation tended to place the Negro man in a position of authority in family relations. The freedmen refused to work in gangs as they had done during

4. Susan Smedes, *A Southern Planter* (Baltimore, 1887), p. 179.

slavery and a man would take his wife and children and rent and operate a farm on his own account.[5] The man or husband in the family was required to sign the rent or work agreements. Sometimes the wives were also required to sign but the husband or father was always held responsible for the behaviour of his family. The more stable elements among the freedmen who had been in a position to assimilate the sentiments and ideas of their former masters soon undertook to buy land. This gave the husband and father an interest in his wife and children that no preaching on the part of white missionaries or Negro preachers could give. But it would be a serious mistake to overlook the manner in which the new economic position of the man was consolidated by the moral support of the Negro church.

There was, of course, moral support for a patriarchal family to be found in the Bible and this fact contributed undoubtedly a holy sanction to the new authority of the Negro man in the family. However, there were more important ways in which the Negro church gave support to Negro family life with the father in a position of authority. As we have pointed out, after Emancipation the Negro had to create a new communal life or become integrated into the communities created by the Negroes who were free before the Civil War. Generally, this resulted in the expansion and complete transformation of these communities. The leaders in creating a new community life were men who with their families worked land or began to buy land or worked as skilled artisans. It is important to observe that these pioneers in the creation of a communal life generally built a church as well as homes. Many of these pioneer leaders were preachers who gathered their communicants about them and became the leaders of the Negro communities. This fact tends to reveal the close relationship between the newly structured life of the Negro and his church organizations.

The churches became and have remained until the past twenty years or so, the most important agency of social control among Negroes. The churches undertook as organizations to censure unconventional and immoral sex behaviour and to punish by expulsion sex offenders and those who violated the

5. See Frazier, *The Negro Family in the United States*, Chapter IX, 'The Downfall of the Matriarchate'.

monogamous *mores*. But it was impossible to change immediately the loose and unregulated sex and family behaviour among a people lacking the institutional basis of European sexual *mores*. Very often the churches had to tolerate or accommodate themselves to sexual irregularities.[6] A bishop in the African Methodist Episcopal Church in recounting the task of 'cleaning up' irregular sex behaviour among the members of the church where he served said that his church became 'the Ecclesiastical Court House, as well as the Church'.[7] Let us not forget, however, the control exercised by the Negro was exercised by dominating personalities. Frequently, they were the preachers who had become leaders of Negroes because of their talents and ability to govern men. Very often they were self-made men.[8] In the Baptist Churches in which the majority of the Negroes have always been concentrated there was even greater opportunity for self-assertion and the assumption of leadership on the part of strong men. This naturally resulted in a pattern of autocratic leadership which has spilled over into most aspects of organized social life among Negroes, especially in as much as many forms of organized social life have grown out of the church and have come under the dominant leadership of Negro preachers.

The Church and Economic Co-operation

As DuBois pointed out more than fifty years ago, 'a study of economic co-operation among Negroes must begin with the Church group'.[9] It was in order to establish their own churches that Negroes began to pool their meagre economic resources and buy buildings and the land on which they stood. As an indication of the small beginnings of these churches, we may

6. In one case of accommodation which was unique only because of the rationalization which the Negroes used to reconcile their habitual unregulated sex behaviour with Christian morality regarding premarital sex relations, the Negroes evolved the doctrine of 'clean sheets'. According to this 'doctrine' it was not wrong for two *Christians* to have sex relations outside of marriage since both were 'clean sheets', and could not soil each other as would be the case if one or both were unconverted or sinners.

7. L. J. Coppin, *Unwritten History* (Philadelphia, 1920), p. 127.

8. See Benj. T. Tanner, *An Apology for African Methodism* (Baltimore, 1867), p. 123.

9. W. E. Burghardt DuBois, *Economic Cooperation Among American Negroes* (Atlanta, 1907), p. 54.

note that the value of the property of the African Methodist Episcopal Church in 1787 was only $2,500. During the next century the value of the property of this organization increased to nine million dollars.[10] The Negroes in the other Methodist denominations, and especially in the numerous Baptist Churches, were contributing on a similar scale a part of their small earnings for the construction of churches. At the same time, out of the churches grew mutual aid societies. The earliest society of this type was the Free African Society which was organized in Philadelphia in 1787.[11] We have already noted that the Society was organized by Absalom Jones and Richard Allen, the two Negroes who led the secession from the Methodist Church. At the time the Society was organized, Negroes were migrating to Philadelphia in large numbers and the need for some sort of mutual aid was becoming urgent. The Society became a 'curious sort of ethical and beneficial brotherhood' under the direction of Jones and Allen who exercised a 'parental discipline' over its members. The avowed purpose of this organization was to 'support one another in sickness, and for the benefit of their widows and fatherless children'.

In the cities throughout the United States numerous beneficial societies were organized to provide assistance in time of sickness or death.[12] Many of these beneficial societies, like the Free African Society, were connected with churches. These societies continued to be established throughout the nineteenth century. For example, in Atlanta in 1898 there were nine beneficial societies which had been founded from soon after the Civil War up to 1897.[13] Six of these beneficial societies were connected with churches. The names of these beneficial societies are not without significance. At the Wheat Street Baptist Church, for example, there were two beneficial societies—the

10. *Ibid.*, p. 57.

11. W. E. B. DuBois, *The Philadelphia Negro* (Philadelphia, 1899), pp. 19–20.

12. In 1790 the Brown Fellowship Society was organized among the 'free brown men' of Charleston, South Carolina, to relieve widows and orphans in 'the hour of their distresses, sickness, and death. . . .' The membership of the Society was restricted to fifty persons who paid an admission fee of fifty dollars. See E. Horace Fitchett, 'The Traditions of the Free Negroes in Charleston, South Carolina', *Journal of Negro History*, Vol. 25, pp. 139–52.

13. Du Bois, *Economic Cooperation Among American Negroes*, p. 94.

Rising Star and the Sisters of Love, while at the Bethel (Methodist) Church was the Daughters of Bethel. These associations for mutual aid which were generally known as beneficial societies were often the germ out of which grew the secular insurance companies.

The role of religion and the Negro church in more elementary forms of economic co-operation among Negroes may be seen more clearly in the rural mutual aid societies that sprang up among freedmen after Emancipation. They were formed among the poor, landless Negroes who were thrown upon their own resources. These societies were organized to meet the crises of life—sickness and death; consequently, they were known as 'sickness and burial' societies. The important fact for our study is that these benevolent societies grew out of the Negro church and were inspired by the spirit of Christian charity. They were supported by the pennies which the Negroes could scrape together in order to aid each other in time of sickness but more especially to insure themselves a decent Christian burial. The influence of the simple religious conceptions of the Negro folk and the Bible is revealed in the names of these mutual aid societies which continue to exist in the rural South. They bear such names as 'Love and Charity', 'Builders of the Walls of Jerusalem', 'Sons and Daughters of Esther', 'Brothers and Sisters of Charity', and 'Brothers and Sisters of Love'.[14]

These 'sickness and burial' societies should be distinguished from the fraternal organizations which played an important role in early economic co-operation among Negroes. Fraternal organizations like the Negro Masonic Lodge and the Odd Fellows came into existence among the free Negroes in the North as the result of the influence of the white fraternal organizations.[15] On the other hand, Negroes began before the outbreak of the Civil War to organize fraternal organizations which reflected their own interests and outlook on life. One such secret society, the Knights of Liberty, was organized by a preacher, Reverend Moses Dickson, who was born in Cin-

14. See Arthur Raper, *Preface to Peasantry* (Chapel Hill, 1926), p. 374.
15. See Harold Van Buren Voorhis, P. M., *Negro Masonry in the United States* (New York, 1940), pp. 3–22; and Charles H. Brooks, *A History and Manual of the Grand United Order of Odd Fellows in America* (Philadelphia, 1893), pp. 19–20.

cinnati in 1824.[16] This organization was active in the under-
ground railroad and claimed to have nearly 50,000 members in
1856. Dickson joined the Union Army and after the Civil War
he disbanded the Knights of Liberty. In 1871 he organized
the first Temple and Tabernacle of the Knights and Daughters
of Tabor in Independence, Missouri. The object of this secret
society was 'to help to spread the Christian religion and
education' and its members were advised to 'acquire real
estate, avoid intemperance, and cultivate true manhood'. At
the end of the nineteenth century this society claimed to have
nearly 200,000 members in eighteen jurisdictions scattered
from Maine to California and from the Great Lakes to the
Gulf of Mexico.

The organization and development of the Grand United
Order of True Reformers provides a better example of the
manner in which an organization under the leadership of a
preacher fired with religious zeal played an important role in
economic co-operation and the accumulation of capital. The
founder of the organization was a Reverend Washington
Browne who was born a slave in Georgia in 1849.[17] During the
Civil War he ran away from a new master and made his way
to the North where he received a meagre education. After
Emancipation he returned to Alabama where he joined a
movement of the Good Templars against the whisky ring. But
after observing the various benevolent and burial societies
among Negroes, he decided that Negroes should have a separate
organization adapted to their special needs. In 1876 he
succeeded in bringing together in a single organization, known
as the Grand Fountain of True Reformers, twenty-seven
Fountains with 2,000 members. Although he was not successful
in creating a mutual benefit society, through his paper, *The
Reformer*, he attracted the attention of the Organization of True
Reformers in Virginia. He was invited to Richmond and became the Grand Worthy Master of the Virginia organization.

16. *Why You Should Become a Knight and Daughter of Tabor*, p. 13. Pamphlet
in the Moorland Foundation, Howard University, Washington, D.C.
See also Booker T. Washington, *The Story of the Negro* (New York, 1909),
Vol. II, pp. 158–60.
17. W. P. Burrell and D. E. Johnson, *Twenty-five Years History of the
Grand Fountain of the United Order of True Reformers* (Richmond, Va., 1909),
p. 12.

The True Reformers organized a variety of enterprises, including a weekly newspaper, a real estate firm, a bank, a hotel, a building and loan association, and a grocery and general merchandising store. The True Reformers took the lead in incorporating an insurance feature in its programme for the benefit of its members, an example of which was followed by the other fraternal organizations among Negroes. The insurance ventures failed because they did not have sound actuarial basis and were not under government supervision.[18] Nevertheless, the Negro gained a certain experience and training which prepared him for his more successful business ventures.

The Church and Education

The educational development of Negroes does not reflect to the same extent as their churches and mutual aid associations the racial experience and peculiar outlook on life of Negroes. Education, that is Western or European education, was something totally foreign to the Negro's way of life. This was because, as Woodson has written, 'The first real educators to take up the work of enlightening American Negroes were clergymen interested in the propagation of the gospel among the heathen in the new world.'[19] In fact, the purpose of education was primarily to transmit to the Negro the religious ideas and practices of an alien culture. In the North the strictly religious content of education was supplemented by other elements, whereas in the South limitations were even placed upon enabling the Negro to read the Bible. By 1850 there were large numbers of Negroes attending schools in northern cities. Then, too, individual Negroes managed to acquire a higher education and most of these were men who were preparing to become ministers.

This does not mean that Negroes took no initiative in setting up schools and acquiring an education. The free Negroes in the cities contributed to the support of schools for Negro children. Generally, the support which the free Negroes

18. W. J. Trent, Jr., *Development of Negro Life Insurance Enterprises*, Master's Thesis (University of Pennsylvania, 1932), p. 32.

19. Carter G. Woodson, *The Education of the Negro Prior to 1861* (New York, 1915), p. 18.

provided was greater in southern cities like Baltimore, Washington, and Charleston, South Carolina, than in New York and Philadelphia. As early as 1790, the Brown Fellowship Society in Charleston maintained schools for the free Negro children. An important fact about the schools which the free Negroes maintained was that many of them were Sunday schools. On the eve of the Civil War, 'There were then in Baltimore Sunday schools about 600 Negroes. They had formed themselves into a Bible Association, which had been received into the convention of the Baltimore Bible Society. In 1825 the Negroes there had a day and night school giving courses in Latin and French. Four years later there appeared an "African Free School", with an attendance of from 150 to 175 every Sunday.'[20] Although the Sunday schools represented before the Civil War one of the most important agencies in the education of Negroes, nevertheless the churches through their ministers urged parents to send their children to whatever schools were available.[21]

After Emancipation the initiative on the part of Negroes in providing education for themselves was given a much freer scope. This was because of the great educational crusade which was carried on by northern white missionaries among the freedmen. As the Union armies penetrated the South, the representatives of northern missionary societies and churches sent funds and teachers in the wake of the advancing armies. The majority of the men and women or 'school marms', as they were called, were inspired by a high idealism and faith in the intellectual capacity of Negroes. They laid the foundation for or established most of the Negro colleges in the South. Working with the Freedmen's Bureau which was created by an Act of Congress in 1865 to aid the freedmen in assuming the responsibilities of citizens, they also laid the foundation for a public school system for the newly emancipated Negro. It was Negroes trained in these schools supported by northern churches and philanthropy who became the educated leaders among Negroes.

The schools—elementary, secondary, and those which provided the beginnings of college education—were permeated

20. *Ibid.*, pp. 140–1.
21. See, for example, the resolutions passed by the African Methodist Episcopal Church in 1835 in Grace Naomi Perry, 'The Educational Work of the African Methodist Episcopal Church prior to 1900', unpublished Master's Thesis (Howard University, Washington, D.C., 1948), pp. 15–21.

with a religious and moral outlook. The graduates of these schools went forth as missionaries to raise the moral and religious level of the members of their race. Many of the men were preachers or became preachers. A preacher who was a graduate of a Baptist college founded by white missionaries and who had helped to make the bricks for the buildings of the college, said that when he was graduated, the white president addressed him as follows: 'I want you to go into the worst spot in this State and build a school and a church.'[22] This minister followed the instructions of his white mentor and established the school that provided the primary school and later the only secondary school for Negroes in the country and four Baptist Churches. This is typical of the manner in which the Negro preacher who was often the best educated man in the community took the initiative in establishing schools.

An educated and distinguished bishop in the African Methodist Episcopal Church who was the father of the most distinguished American Negro painter, wrote in his history of the Church in 1867: 'For it is one of the brightest pages in the history of our Church, that while the Army of the Union were forcing their victorious passage through the southern land and striking down treason, the missionaries of our Church in the persons of Brown, Lynch, Cain, Handy, Stanford, Steward, and others, were following in their wake and establishing the Church and the school house. . . .'[23] The work of the Negro preacher in establishing schools was especially important since the southern States provided only a pittance of public funds for the education of Negro children. When the Julius Rosenwald Fund contributed to the building of more than 5,000 schools for Negroes in the South in order to stimulate the public authorities to appropriate money for Negro schools, Negro churches played an important role in making possible the schools aided by the Rosenwald Fund. Negroes contributed 17 per cent of the total cost of the schools which amounted to over $28,000,000. They raised much of their share in this amount through church suppers and programmes under the auspices of their churches.[24]

22. Secured during an interview.
23. Tanner, *An Apology for African Methodism*, p. 251.
24. Frazier, *The Negro in the United States*, p. 429.

The impetus among Negroes to build institutions of higher education was due primarily to their need for an educated ministry. But the desire on the part of the masses for an educated ministry was far from universal. The masses of Negroes were still impressed by the ignorant and illiterate minister who often boasted that he had not been corrupted by wicked secular learning. Soon after the 'invisible institution' of the slaves was integrated into the institutional church, it was feared that a schism would occur in the African Methodist Episcopal Church as the result of the conflict between the ignorant and intelligent elements in the church.[25] Nevertheless, the African Methodist Episcopal Church succeeded in establishing a number of so-called colleges and universities.[26] The African Methodist Episcopal Zion Church and the Colored Methodist Episcopal Church also established schools. The Baptists had to depend upon local efforts. In South Carolina the Negro Baptists who became dissatisfied with the white control of the college for Negroes finally established their own school.[27]

The schools and colleges maintained by the Negro church denominations have never attained a high level as educational institutions. They have generally nurtured a narrow religious outlook and have restricted the intellectual development of Negroes even more than the schools established for Negroes by the white missionaries. This has been due only partly to lack of financial resources. It hardly needs to be emphasized that there was no intellectual tradition among Negroes to sustain colleges and universities. The attendance of Negro students at private colleges has reflected the social stratification of the Negro community. The children of the upper class in the Negro community have generally attended the schools established by the Congregational Church and the better type of schools supported by the white Methodists and Baptists for Negroes. Nevertheless, the Negro church has affected the entire intellectual development and outlook of Negroes. This has been due both to the influence of the Negro church which has permeated every phase of social life and to the influence of the

25. See Woodson, *The History of the Negro Church*, p. 172.
26. See Perry, *op. cit., passim.*
27. Stephen C. Campbell, 'The Influence of Negro Baptists on Secondary Education in South, Carolina', unpublished Master's Essay (Wayne University, Detroit, Mich., 1947).

Negro preacher whose authoritarian personality and anti-intellectualism has cast a shadow over the intellectual outlook of Negroes.

An Arena of Political Life

It was inevitable that preachers who had played such an important role in the organized social life of Negroes should become political leaders during the Reconstruction period when the Negro enjoyed civil rights.[28] The career of Bishop Henry M. Turner of the African Methodist Episcopal Church will enable us to see how these leaders in the religious life of Negroes became, after Emancipation, leaders in politics. He was born in South Carolina of free ancestry in 1834.[29] On his mother's side he was the grandson of an African prince. He was able to acquire some education through private instruction. When fourteen years of age he joined the Methodist Church and later became a chaplain in the United States Army. After the Civil War he transferred to the African Methodist Episcopal Church in which he advanced from a position of an itinerant preacher to that of an elder. During this time he became active in politics. He organized Negroes in the Republican Party in Georgia and was elected to the Georgia legislature. Turner was expelled from the Georgia legislature when 'white supremacy' was restored in Georgia and as the result of persecution he was forced to resign as postmaster of Macon, Georgia, a position to which he had been appointed by President Grant. Turner abandoned politics and devoted his life to the Church.

During the Reconstruction period a number of outstanding leaders in the Baptist and in the other Methodist denominations became outstanding as leaders of Negroes in politics. Bishop James W. Hood of the African Methodist Episcopal Zion Church was elected president of a convention of Negroes in North Carolina which was perhaps the first political convention called by Negroes after they gained their freedom. He served as a local magistrate and later as a Deputy Collector of Internal Revenue for the United States.[30] Hood was also appointed

28. See Woodson, *The History of the Negro Church*, Chapter XI, 'The Call of Politics'.
29. Henry M. Turner, *Life and Times of Henry M. Turner* (Atlanta, 1917), p. 23.
30. Woodson, *The History of the Negro Church*, pp. 236–8.

Assistant Superintendent of Public Instruction of the State of North Carolina. These ministers who became the political leaders of Negroes were all Republicans and shared on the whole the conservative political philosophy of that party.

It should be noted that of the twenty Negroes elected to the House of Representatives of the United States from the South during the Reconstruction period only two were preachers, but one of the two Negroes who were elected to the Senate was a preacher.[31] Senator Hiram R. Revels, one of the two Negroes elected from Mississippi, was born a free Negro in North Carolina in 1822. He moved to the North and was ordained in the African Methodist Episcopal Church. When the Civil War broke out he assisted in organizing two Negro regiments in Maryland. He worked with the Freedmen's Bureau and, like other preachers, engaged in the establishment of churches and schools before entering politics in Mississippi. Revel's career in politics, like that of other Negro preachers, was of short duration because of the re-establishment of white supremacy in the South. After elimination from politics in the South, the Negro preachers generally devoted themselves to their church though in some cases they became heads of Negro schools.

As the result of the elimination of Negroes from the political life of the American community, the Negro church became the arena of their political activities. The church was the main area of social life in which Negroes could aspire to become the leaders of men. It was the area of social life where ambitious individuals could achieve distinction and the symbols of status. The church was the arena in which the struggle for power and the thirst for power could be satisfied. This was especially important to Negro men who had never been able to assert themselves and assume the dominant male role, even in family relations, as defined by American culture. In the Baptist churches, with their local autonomy, individual Negro preachers ruled their followers in an arbitrary manner, while the leaders in the hierarchy of the various Methodist denominations were czars, rewarding and punishing their subordinates on the basis of personal loyalties. Moreover, the monetary

31. Samuel D. Smith, *The Negro Congress, 1870–1901* (Chapel Hill, 1940), p. 8.

rewards which went with power were not small when one considers the contributions of millions of Negroes and the various business activities of the churches.

The Negro church was not only an arena of political life for the leaders of Negroes, it had a political meaning for the masses. Although they were denied the right to vote in the American community, within their Churches, especially the Methodist Churches, they could vote and engage in electing their officers. The elections of bishops and other officers and representatives to conventions has been a serious activity for the masses of Negroes. But, in addition, the church had a political significance for Negroes in a broader meaning of the term. The development of the Negro church after Emancipation was tied up, as we have seen, largely with the Negro family. A study of Negro churches in a Black Belt county in Georgia in 1903 revealed, for example, that a large proportion of the churches were 'family churches'.[32] Outside of the family, the church represented the only other organized social existence. The rural Negro communities in the South were named after their churches. In fact, the Negro population in the rural South has been organized in 'church communities' which represented their widest social orientation and the largest social groups in which they found an identification. Moreover, since the Negro was an outsider in the American community, it was the church that enlisted his deepest loyalties. Therefore, it was more than an amusing incident to note some years ago in a rural community in Alabama, that a Negro when asked to identify the people in the adjoining community replied: 'The nationality in there is Methodist'. We must remember that these people have no historic traditions and language and sentiments to identify them as the various nationalities of Europe. For the Negro masses, in their social and moral isolation in American society, the Negro church community has been a nation within a nation.

A Refuge in a Hostile White World

In providing a structured social life in which the Negro could give expression to his deepest feeling and at the same time achieve status and find a meaningful existence, the Negro

32. DuBois, *The Negro Church*, p. 57.

church provided a refuge in a hostile white world. For the slaves who worked and suffered in an alien world, religion offered a means of catharsis for their pent-up emotions and frustrations. Moreover, it turned their minds from the sufferings and privations of this world to a world after death where the weary would find rest and the victims of injustices would be compensated. The Negroes who were free before the Civil War found status in the church which shielded them from the contempt and discriminations of the white world. Then for a few brief years after Emancipation the hopes and expectations of the black freedmen were raised and they thought that they would have acceptance and freedom in the white man's world. But their hopes and expectations were rudely shattered when white supremacy was re-established in the South. They were excluded from participation in the white man's world except on the basis of inferiority. They were disfranchised and the public schools provided for them were a mere travesty on education. The courts set up one standard of justice for the white and another standard for the black man. They were stigmatized as an inferior race lacking even the human attributes which all men are supposed to possess. They were subjected to mob violence involving lynchings and burnings alive which were justified even by the white Christian churches.

Where could the Negro find a refuge from this hostile white world? They remembered from their Bible that the friends of Job had counselled him to curse God and die. They remembered too that Samson when blinded had torn down the Temple and destroyed himself along with his tormentors. Had not one of their leading ministers in his disillusionment and despair cried out against the flag of the nation he had served in the Civil War, 'I don't want to die under the dirty rag'. But the Negro masses did not curse God and die.[33] They could not pull down the Temple upon the white man and themselves. They retained their faith in God and found a refuge in their churches.

The Negro church with its own forms of religious worship was a world which the white man did not invade but only regarded with an attitude of condescending amusement. The

33. The suicide rate among Negroes, it may be noted here, has always been much lower than among whites.

Negro church could enjoy this freedom so long as it offered no threat to the white man's dominance in both economic and social relations. And, on the whole, the Negro's church was not a threat to white domination and aided the Negro to become accommodated to an inferior status. The religion of the Negro continued to be other-worldly in its outlook, dismissing the privations and sufferings and injustices of this world as temporary and transient.[34] The Negro church remained a refuge despite the fact that the Negro often accepted the disparagement of Negroes by whites and the domination of whites.[35] But all of this was a part of God's plan and was regarded just as the physical environment was regarded. What mattered was the way he was treated in the church which gave him an opportunity for self-expression and status. Since the Negro was not completely insulated from the white world and had to conform to some extent to the ways of white men, he was affected by their evaluation of him. Nevertheless, he could always find an escape from such, often painful, experiences within the shelter of his church.

34. See Charles S. Johnson, *Shadow of the Plantation* (Chicago, 1934), Chapter V, for description of Negro church services and sermons of Negro preachers in rural Black Belt County in Alabama. See also J. Mason Brewer, *The Word on the Brazos* (Austin, Tex., 1953), for Negroes' reaction to their preachers.

35. It is very likely that in the minds of the simple rural Negroes, the image of God conformed to that of a kindly white planter. The writer heard a Negro preacher in rural Alabama declare in a sermon that 'Pharaoh was a "nigger" and like all niggers who get power he oppressed the Jews who were God's chosen people'.

CHAPTER 4

Negro Religion in the City

The Migration to Cities

THE migrations of Negroes to cities, especially to northern
cities, produced a crisis in the life of the Negro similar in
many respects to the crisis created by the Civil War and
Emancipation. Immediately following Emancipation, Negroes
drifted into the cities of the South in larger numbers propor-
tionately than the whites. Then, after a decade or so, there was
an almost imperceptible drift of the Negroes to hundreds of
southern cities until the First World War when the mass
migrations of Negroes to northern cities was set in motion.
Until the First World War about nine-tenths of the Negroes
were still in the South and about four-fifths of those in the
South lived in rural areas. The War created an unprecedented
demand on the part of northern industries for workers, especially large numbers of unskilled workers. The War had cut off
the immigration of workers from Europe and many immigrant
workers returned to Europe in order to fight for their home-
lands. The mass movement of Negroes from the South was
stimulated also by floods and the ravages of the boll weevil as
well as the oppression which Negroes had suffered. As the
result of the mass movements from the South large Negro
communities were created in the metropolitan areas of the
North. Although the movements slowed down after the War,
Negroes continued to migrate to the cities of the North and
during the Second World War southern Negroes were attracted
by the war industries to the cities of the West. Negroes have
continued to move into southern cities as well as into the cities
of the North and West, with the result that nearly two-thirds
of the Negroes in the country as a whole live under urban
conditions.

The movement of Negroes to cities, we have said, created a
crisis similar to that resulting from Emancipation. It was a crisis
in that it uprooted the masses of Negroes from their customary

way of life, destroying the social organization which represented both an accommodation to conditions in the rural South and an accommodation to their segregated and inferior status in southern society. In the city environment the family of the masses of Negroes from rural areas, which lacked an institutional basis and was held together only by co-operation in making a living or by sympathies and sentiments generated by living together in the same household, was unable to stand the shock of the disintegrating forces in urban life. Often men who went ahead to the cities with firm resolve to send for their wives and children acquired new interests and never sent for their families. Even when families migrated to the cities, they often disintegrated when they no longer had the support of friends and neighbours and the institutions which had held together families in the rural South. As a result there were many footloose men and homeless women in the cities who had broken all family ties. Moreover, since the women in families were required to work as well as the men, the children were no longer subject to family discipline. The disorganization of the Negro family in the city was reflected in the large numbers of women who had been deserted by their husbands, by the increased numbers of unmarried mothers, and by the high rate of juvenile delinquency among Negroes.

In the cold impersonal environment of the city, the institutions and associations which had provided security and support for the Negro in the rural environment could not be resurrected. The mutual aid or 'sickness and burial' societies could no longer provide security during the two major crises which the Negroes feared most. In fact, in the crowded slums of northern cities, neighbourliness and friendship no longer had any meaning. The Negro could not find even the warmth and sympathy of the secret fraternal organizations which had added colour and ornament to a drab existence in the South.

The most important crisis in the life of the Negro migrant was produced by the absence of the church which had been the centre of his social life and a refuge from a hostile white world. The Negro church, as we have seen, was not only the organization that had created cohesion among the slaves but it was also the basis of organized life among the Negroes who were free before the Civil War and among the freedmen following

Emancipation. Moreover, it had set the pattern for organized
social life among Negroes. We are interested in discovering how
the breakdown of the traditional social organization of Negro
life in the city resulted in the transformation of the Negro
church and changed the religious behaviour of Negroes.

The Secularization of the Churches

In the urban environment the entire mental outlook of
Negroes was changed. This was especially true with the migrants
who went to the large metropolitan centres and industrial cities
of the North. In the strange environment the Negro endea-
voured to explain his new experiences in terms of his traditional
outlook on life which was saturated with his religion and the
image of the world provided by his knowledge of the Bible.
This is shown vividly in the letters which the migrants sent
home to their families often through the pastor of the church to
which they belonged in the South.[1] In one letter a migrant to
Pittsburgh undertook to describe the marvel of the gigantic
blazing steel furnaces by writing that they were just like what
would happen on Judgment Day. But the new experiences
could not be contained in the traditional ways of thinking
about the world. Even the illiterate migrants could not remain
unaffected by the new ideas and above all the new ways of
behaving in the urban environment. They were impressed by
the new status in which they found themselves. They marvelled
at the fact that their children went to school with white children
and the white teachers addressed them as Mister and Mistress.
They saw Negroes in unaccustomed roles as policemen and
firemen and in positions of trust and authority and that
Negroes could vote as white men did. Through these experiences they acquired a new conception of Negroes and of themselves.

The change in status was related in part to the fact that in the
northern city the Negro children received the same education
as the white child even when they were not in the same school
with whites. The education was of a nature to broaden their
intellectual horizon and give them an entirely new outlook on

---

1. 'Letters of Negro Migrants of 1916–1918', *Journal of Negro History*,
Vol. IV (1919), pp. 290–340; and 'Additional Letters of Negro Migrants',
ibid., pp. 412–65.

life. In addition, education opened the door to many occupations that had been closed to Negroes on account of race in the South. As a consequence there was an acceleration of the occupational differentiation of the Negro population in northern cities. Whereas, for example, preachers constituted about fifty per cent of the professional class among Negroes in the South, in northern cities, where nearly nine-tenths of the Negroes in the North lived, only one professional Negro in ten was a preacher. And what was important, Negroes were not only to be found in most of the occupational groups in the northern cities but Negro professional men and women and white-collar workers were not confined to the Negro community as in the South.

On the basis of the occupational differentiation of the Negro population, a new system of social stratification or socio-economic classes came into existence. We have noted the simple stratification of the Negro community in the South which consisted of a small upper class based largely upon family and a light complexion and later based to some degree upon education. As a result of the entrance of Negroes into new occupations, some of whom served the new needs of the large Negro communities in northern cities, a new class structure emerged consisting of three major classes.[2] This new class system has not only helped to change the traditional organization of Negro life but it has caused the Negro church to adapt itself to the general outlook and religious requirements of the different classes.

From the standpoint of formal affiliation with the various denominations, it appears from available statistics that the Negro in the northern city continued his traditional affiliation. That is to say, nearly two-thirds of the Negroes continued to attend Baptist churches and about a third were in the various Methodist churches. Most of the remainder of the Negroes who were affiliated with the church were in the Episcopal and Presbyterian churches, and a small number in the Roman Catholic Church. But these figures fail to tell what had occurred in the Negro churches and in the religious behaviour of Negroes. The change which occurred can be best described as a seculari-

2. See St. Clair Drake and Horace R. Cayton, *Black Metropolis* (New York, 1945), Part III.

zation of the Negro churches. By secularization we mean that the Negro churches lost their predominantly other-worldly outlook and began to focus attention upon the Negro's condition in this world. The most obvious evidence of secularization has been that the churches have been forced to tolerate card playing and dancing and theatre-going. The opposition to these forms of recreation was rationalized on the basis that they would lead to gambling and immorality rather than that they were sinful.[3]

A more important indication of the growing secularization of Negro churches has been their interest in the affairs of the community.[4] The interest in the affairs of the community included recreational work and contributions to the work of a social welfare agency like the National Urban League or organizations fighting for civil rights like the National Association for the Advancement of Colored People. This new direction of interest in worldly affairs was more strongly indicated by the nature of the sermons of the ministers and their leadership in political affairs in which their church members actively participated.[5] In a number of northern cities the pastors of large Negro churches have been influential in politics and have received important political appointments.[6] It is no accident that one of the four Negro members of the House of Representatives of the United States is a preacher, the Reverend Adam Clayton Powell, the pastor of the Abyssinian Baptist Church in New York City which is reported to be the largest church in the United States. Reverend Powell has not only been a political leader of Negroes but he has also marched with them in the boycott of stores which refused to employ Negroes.

The secularization of the Negro church has not affected to

3. See Benjamin E. Mays and Joseph W. Nicholson, *The Negro's Church* (New York, 1933), p. 156.

4. See *ibid.*, pp. 154 ff.

5. In an analysis of 100 sermons Mays and Nicholson found that 26 dealt with practical affairs, 54 were predominantly other worldly, and 20 were highly doctrinal. Mays and Nicholson, *op. cit.*, p. 59. Since this study was made in 1933, there is every indication that the percentage of practical sermons has increased.

6. The pastor of a large Baptist church in Philadelphia, the Reverend Marshall Sheppard, was appointed by President Franklin D. Roosevelt as Recorder of Deeds for the District of Columbia.

the same extent and in the same manner all sections of the Negro population. The manner in which secularization has affected Negroes is related to the new stratification of the Negro population. In a study of stratification in Negro churches in Chicago, it was found that church-going was not important for many persons of upper-class status and that those who attended church attended churches with services that were ritualistic and deliberative, the Episcopal, Presbyterian, and Congregational.[7] The upper middle class was found to be affiliated with the same churches as the upper class with the important difference, however, that the upper middle class was more faithful in church attendance. Some members of the upper middle class also attended the Methodist and Baptist churches for social reasons. On the other hand, the members of the lower middle class were affiliated with churches which were described as semi-demonstrative, as there was emotional participation on the part of the members. This was indicative of their recent social ascension from the lower class for whom demonstrative participation in the church services is regarded as indispensable. In fact, some of the members of the lower middle class preferred to attend certain Methodist and Baptist churches for this very reason.

In the cities of the North the churches were much larger than the churches in the South. The average membership of a Negro church in the North was close to 800 while the average for the South was less than half that number.[8] The Negro preacher in the northern city has striven to build up large churches which are a measure of his status and influence, not to mention his control of economic resources. These churches are vast social organizations with a number of departments concerned with many aspects of Negro life other than the religious. They have established systems of book-keeping and something approaching an impersonal bureaucratic organization. In spite of the wealth and power of these churches, they repel the Negro masses who seek a type of religious association that is warm and intimate and in which they have a satisfactory status.

7. Vattel E. Daniel, 'Ritual and Stratification in Chicago Negro Churches', *American Sociological Review*, Vol. 7, p. 359.
8. See Mays and Nicholson, *op. cit.*, p. 107.

Religion in the 'Storefront' Church

The inadequacy, from a religious standpoint, of the institutional denominations accounts for the 'storefront' churches which one finds in Negro communities in American cities. In the survey of Negro churches in twelve cities, to which we have referred, out of a total of 2,104 church buildings, 777 were 'storefront' churches or houses and the remainder were conventional church buildings.[9] These 'storefront' churches, as the name suggests, are generally conducted in unrented or abandoned stores, though some may. be found in run-down houses. They are located in the poorer and deteriorated areas of Negro communities. They often owe their existence to the initiative on the part of a 'Jack-leg' preacher, that is, a semiliterate or an uneducated preacher, who gathers about him the poorer Negroes who seek a religious leader in the city. Nearly a half of 777 'storefront' churches in the study referred to above were Baptist and a somewhat smaller number were known as Holiness and Spiritualist churches. There were less than ten churches identified with any of the three regularly established Methodist denominations though many of the members of these 'storefront' churches had been in Methodist churches.

The 'storefront' church represents an attempt on the part of the migrants, especially from the rural areas of the South, to re-establish a type of church in the urban environment to which they were accustomed. They want a church, first of all, in which they are known as people. In the large city church they lose their identity completely and, as many of the migrants from the rural South have said, neither the church members nor the pastor know them personally. Sometimes they complain with bitterness that the pastor of the large city church knows them only as the number on the envelope in which they place their dues. In wanting to be treated as human beings, they want status in the church which was the main or only organization in the South in which they had status. Some of the statements concerning their reason for leaving the big denominational churches was that 'back home in the South' they had a seat in the church that everyone recognized as theirs and that

9. Mays and Nicholson, *op. cit.*, p. 313.

if the seat were empty on Sunday the pastor came to their homes to find out the cause of their absence.

The desire for the warm and intimate association of fellow worshippers in church services was not the only reason why the 'storefront' church was more congenial to the recently urbanized Negro than the cold impersonal atmosphere of the large denominational city church. In these small 'storefront' churches the Negro migrant could worship in a manner to which he had been accustomed. The sermon by the pastor is of a type to appeal to traditional ideas concerning hell and heaven and the imagery which the Negro has acquired from the Bible. Much emphasis is placed upon sins of the flesh, especially sexual sins. The preacher leads the singing of the Spirituals and other hymns with which the Negroes with a folk background are acquainted. The singing is accompanied by 'shouting' or holy dancing which permits the maximum of free religious expression on the part of the participants.

In the cities of the North and even in the cities in the South, these 'storefront' churches are constantly being organized by all kinds of so-called preachers in order to attract lower-class Negroes. During the 1920s when southern Negroes were flocking to Harlem in New York City, it was found that only 54 out of 140 churches in Harlem were housed in regular church structures.[10] The remainder were of the 'storefront' type which had been organized by preachers, many of whom were exploiters and charlatans. They based their appeal on the Negro's desire to find salvation in the next world and to escape from sickness and the insecurities of this world. One of these churches advertised:

> We Believe that all Manner of Disease Can Be Cured
> Jesus is the Doctor
> Services on Sunday.[11]

The large number of churches in Negro communities in the North as well as in the South has raised the question as to whether the Negro population is over-churched.[12] There is no

---

10. Ira de A. Reid, 'Let Us Prey!' *Opportunity*, Vol. 4 (September 1926), pp. 274–8.
11. *Ibid.*, p. 275.
12. See Mays and Nicholson, *op. cit.*, Chapter XVI.

way of answering this question and it is irrelevant in a sense
when one considers the important role of the Negro church in
the organization of the Negro community. The vast majority of
Negroes have constituted a lower class, gaining a living as common labourers and in domestic and personal service. Among
these people there is little associational life and the churches of
all types represent, as we have seen, the main form of organized
social life. Even when Negroes have broken away from the
traditional churches they have sought in new religious groups
a way of life which would conform to their needs. This may be
seen when we turn to consider the cults which have grown up
in recent years among Negroes.

Negro Cults in the City

The cults which have developed among Negroes represent
something new in the religious life of Negroes. They are sometimes not differentiated from the traditional religious groups
which meet in abandoned stores and houses because the cults
often meet in the same type of buildings. In most of the 'storefront' churches the Negro maintains his traditional beliefs and
conceptions of God and the world and himself. On the other
hand, in the new cults which flourish in the cities, Negroes have
abandoned their traditional notions about God and the world
and, what is of crucial importance, their conceptions of themselves. An attempt has been made to classify the different types
of cults from the standpoint of such features as faith healing or
holiness or whether they claim an Islamic origin,[13] but there is
much overlapping. Moreover, while all these cults represent
'New Gods of the City',[14] there is an important difference
between those which seek to restore a purer form of Christianity
or sanctification and holiness and those which tend to be secular
in outlook and represent primarily a complete transformation
of the Negro as a race. Of course, in some of those cults in
which the Negro escapes from his racial identity, there may be
faith healing and sanctification but these are subordinate to
the main orientation of the cults.

13. See the classification in Raymond J. Jones, *A Comparative Study of
Religious Cult Behavior Among Negroes with Special Reference to Emotional Condi-
tioning Factors*, Master's Thesis (Howard University, Washington, D.C.,
1939), pp. 3–6.
14. See Drake and Cayton, *op. cit.*, pp. 641–6.

We shall begin with the cults which seek to restore a purer form of Christianity through the sanctification of their members. In Chicago, 107 of the 475 churches were Holiness churches and 51 Spiritualist.[15] The Holiness churches are composed of people who seek to restore the church as it was given to the Saints. The chief religious activity of the members of the Holiness cults is that form of ecstatic worship which is known as 'getting happy' or 'shouting'. This frenzied behaviour is often accompanied by drums, guitars, or tambourines. The worship in these Holiness churches is the type of behaviour which Daniel studied in the nine ecstatic cults.[16] They insist that Christians shall live free of sin and in a state of holiness. They refuse to compromise with the sinful ways of the world. By sin they mean the use of tobacco, the drinking of alcoholic beverages, cursing and swearing, dancing, playing cards, and adultery. All of such activities are regarded as 'carnal-mindedness'.[17] In recounting their achievement of a state of holiness, some members tell of having visions of heaven. They claim, as a pastor of a Holiness church said, that they 'are the common ordinary people that Jesus dwelt among'.[18]

One of these Holiness churches in Philadelphia was founded by a woman, known as Bishop Ida Robinson, who was born in Florida and grew up in Georgia.[19] She was converted at the age of seventeen and became active in the church. However, she left the South and went to Philadelphia where she founded the Mt. Sinai Holy Church in 1924. Bishop Robinson is described as 'tall, sharp of feature and eye, medium brown in colour, probably of mixed Indian-Negro blood. Her education has been limited, but she is extremely intelligent, and a competent leader. She is, of course, a keen student of the Bible.'[20] She acquired the building for her church from a white Pentecostal congregation. She is the supreme head of the cult because, as she claims, her authority comes directly from God. She has ordained a woman as vice-bishop and a number of

15. *Ibid.*, p. 633.
16. *Op. cit.*, pp. 357–8.
17. Drake and Cayton, *op. cit.*, p. 637.
18. Quoted in *ibid.*, p. 639.
19. See Arthur Huff Fauset, *Black Gods of the Metropolis* (Philadelphia, 1944), Chapter II.
20. *Ibid.*, p. 14.

elders and preachers who are heads of member churches in other cities.

Membership in this church is determined by a period of testing which 'is known as sanctification, and an experience, usually speaking in tongues, which is the sign that one has been filled with the Holy Spirit'.[21] After one becomes a member one may join the Preachers' Class in which one is drilled in the Bible and 'spiritual wisdom'. Financial support of the church is provided through tithes and collections taken at the services when the bishop leads the members to the collection table. At these services there is singing and the clapping of hands after which there are testimonies. These testimonies tell of God's having guided these witnesses to the power of Holy Spirit in healing ills of the body. The sermon by the bishop which consists of attacks upon the sins of this world which is approaching its end, results in the rising of individuals who become frenzied as they speak in tongues and engage in 'shouting'. After the bishop leaves or rests, there are other services which culminate in a communion service during which they drink grape juice and are served crackers. The practices of the church include the tabooing of divorce and marriage outside the circle of members. Men and women may show sentiment toward each other only when they plan to marry. Women are required to dress in a 'holy' manner which means wearing plain black or white dresses and stockings, preferably of cotton, and if men wear neckties they must be plain white or black.

The most important and most widely known of the Holiness cults is the Father Divine Peace Mission Movement.[22] Little is known of the history of Father Divine before 1919 when he acquired a modest cottage in Sayville, New Jersey, in response to an advertisement that one or two German-Americans, who still continued to fight the Great War, would sell even to 'coloured buyers'. Major J. Divine, as he signed his name, and 'Pinninah', his wife, opened a free employment bureau but soon began to take in the destitute and feed them. During the next ten years or so people flocked in increasing numbers to the house for religious services and 'Reverend' Divine became 'Father'

21. *Ibid.*, p. 15.
22. See Robert A. Parker, *The Incredible Messiah* (Boston, 1937), and Fauset, *op. cit.*, Chapter VI.

Divine. He added rooms to the house, which began to be known as 'Heaven', as the number of people came to 'lift their voices in praise of Father Divine'. The visitors were impressed by the sumptuous feasts which were served after Father Divine had blessed every dish. Legends began to grow concerning the unlimited wealth of Father Divine and his miraculous powers of healing. Those who listened at the shaded windows 'were shocked by ejaculations in which rapture and pain were intermingled with cries of "Thank you, Father".'[23]

It was not long before the attention of the public authorities was called to the fact that women were living in the 'Heaven'. Moreover, the white residents complained about the noise and the motley throng of men and women who were attracted to these emotional orgies. Divine became a sort of martyr when he and his followers were arrested and he was indicted for maintaining a public nuisance. When Divine refused to co-operate with authorities his case was taken before Justice Lewis J. Smith of the Supreme Court of Nassau County, a Presbyterian who was disgusted that educated white men and women should testify that they believed Divine was the 'personified perfection' of God. Divine was found guilty by a jury and sentenced to jail. Within less than a week after Divine's conviction, Justice Smith died unexpectedly. It was this event that set on Father Divine the seal of omnipotence in the eyes of his followers. Divine was released from jail on bail during an appeal to the Appellate Court which reversed the ruling of Judge Smith. In Harlem at a mass meeting characterized by shouting and singing where white women as well as black sought to kiss his hand there occurred 'the apotheosis, the deification of the man who acclaimed himself Father Divine'.[24]

Father Divine's Peace Mission Movement is distinguished from other cults first by the fact that Father Divine is the organization and that all directions are issued by him. This follows logically from the fact that Father Divine is God.[25] He is surrounded by secretaries, the majority of whom are white and Negro women, who record everything he says and transmit his orders to his followers. His intimate participation in every

23. Parker, *op. cit.*, p. 9.
24. See *ibid.*, p. 30.
25. Fauset, *op. cit.*, pp. 56 ff.

activity is indicated by his role at the banquet table or Holy
Communion, where every dish passes through his hands, he
pours the first glass of water, cuts the first slice of cake, and
places the serving spoon in each container. Certain figures are
close to Divine, one being his personal secretary and the other
his wife, known as Mother Divine. Everything done, even in
other cities, must meet with his approval and he meets scores
of his followers daily from far and near. His followers have been
estimated from thousands to several millions but nobody knows
the actual number. Nor is it easy to ascertain how membership
is attained. It appears that one type of member is the person
who subscribes to the beliefs and practices and attends service
and the other has renounced the world completely and joins the
'kingdom' after disposing of his worldly goods according to
instructions. He becomes completely subject to the will of
Father Divine. This is all tied up with the question of the support of the movement, a question which no one has been able
to answer.[26]

Another important feature of this cult is that it does not
tolerate any form of racial discrimination. Wherever Negroes
and whites live together, they are required to eat and sleep
together.[27] This may account for the fact that the movement
has not spread into the South. At the same time it has been
suggested that the strict sexual taboos are designed to meet the
eventuality that the movement may spread into the South.
Nevertheless, after Mother Divine died, Father Divine married
a young white woman about twenty-two years of age, who has
become the new Mother Divine. The sex taboo forbids man and
wife to live together. When a married couple enter the cult,
they become brother and sister and can have no relations with
the opposite sex. Even dancing with members of the opposite
sex is forbidden.

Although intoxicants are strictly forbidden, there are no food
taboos. And what is more important, business enterprises are

26. It appears that some Negroes have given up their meagre savings
when they entered the 'kingdom' or 'Heaven'. But it is likely that Father
Divine has received more substantial support from white people. The
Internal Revenue Service, it seems, has never been able to discover the
source of income of Father Divine who, being God, is supposed to own
everything in the world.
27. Fauset, *op. cit.*, pp. 61, 66.

encouraged. In fact, the movement publishes a weekly periodical, *New Day*, which is the sacred text of the organization rather than the Bible. Father Divine discourages the reading of the Bible. *New Day* contains every speech uttered by Father Divine. It also carries advertisements of many large and well-known commercial enterprises. Every advertisement carries within its text the injunction: 'Peace' and sometimes adds 'Thank you, Father'. The use of such words as Negro and white is forbidden. A single copy of *New Day* may contain 132 pages filled, with the exception of the advertisements, with the words and activities of Father Divine.

The followers of Father Divine believe that he is God and that he will never die. To them God has appeared as a Negro because the Negro is the lowliest of God's creatures and God prefers to bring salvation to the lowly. The followers of Father Divine are not to refer to the passage of time, as for example, age. A true follower of Father Divine will never die and illness means that he has strayed from the faith. Death represents the culmination of the failure to live according to the faith. When faced with difficulty, the faithful need only to say, 'Thank you, Father'.

Father Divine made his triumphant entrance into Harlem during the first half of 1932 at the depth of the Great Depression. To hungry Harlem, 'The real God is the God who feeds us'.[28] Ten years later, Father Divine, though God, fled from New York City to Philadelphia in order to avoid a number of embarrassing lawsuits. There ensued a struggle for the spiritual control of the Negro masses in Harlem.[29] The two contenders were Elder Lightfoot Solomon Michaux, a former fish peddler, whose disciples call him the 'Happy Am I Prophet', and the other was Mother Rosa Artimus Horne, a former seamstress, described as the 'Pray for Me Priestess'. One investigator has written as follows: 'While sharing a mutual dislike for each other, the two oracles have many things in common. Both operate five temples throughout the nation; claim to be miraculous healers; profess national radio and sawdust trail followings numbering in the hundreds of thousands; are coy about reveal-

28. Parker, *op. cit.*, pp. 58–9.
29. Frank Rasky, 'Harlem's Religious Zealots', *Tomorrow*, Vol. 9 (November, 1949), pp. 11–17.

ing the exact amount of their earnings; and both are adroit showmen who harbour contempt for the methods of Father Divine.'[30] Elder Michaux has a larger popular appeal and has been able to enhance his prestige by association with important public leaders. He has had mass baptisms in the Griffith Stadium in Washington, where two hundred white-robed candidates are immersed in water from the Potomac River. His sermons consist chiefly of tirades against sin, rowdy women, slot machines, whisky, beer, and gamblers. He is reputed to be a millionaire and keeps a retinue of servants, including cooks, valets, maids for his wife, and chauffeurs to drive his eight large automobiles. He has much influence among some government officials who regard him as a spokesman for many Negro church people.

Mother Horne, who lacked the humour of Elder Michaux, carried on a grim evangelism of the fire and brimstone variety.[31] She claimed to have raised thousands of people from the dead besides having made hundreds of the blind see. In their religious services the members of Mother Horne's cult are stimulated by clapping their hands to maddening rhythms accompanied by a piano and a drum. They generally give testimonies to the powers of Mother Horne while she illuminates these testimonies with such remarks as 'punching the devil in the eye'. She was reputed to have had properties worth millions of dollars which enabled her and her daughter to live well.

The recent death in 1960 of Bishop Charles Emmanuel Grace, better known as 'Daddy' Grace, has brought to the attention of the American people a cult leader of considerable influence who possessed a considerable fortune. He was a man of mixed parentage, Negro and Portuguese, who came to the United States around 1920. He is said to have worked as a cook in the railway service before he began to preach in 1925.[32] He founded an organization known as the United House of Prayer for All People with churches in twenty or more cities along the eastern seaboard. Bishop Grace, with his flowing hair, was the undisputed head of the United House of Prayer. All moneys had to be returned to Grace in his office in Washington.

30. *Ibid.*, p. 11.
31. *Ibid.*, p. 14.
32. Fauset, *op. cit.*, p. 26.

Membership in this organization was supposed to be based upon a special religious experience, but membership seemed to be open to anyone. There was considerable emphasis upon the money with the result that numerous collections were taken during the services. This cult is essentially a sect of the holiness type, including conversion, sanctification, and the usual taboos. According to Fauset, 'the beliefs boil down to a worship of Daddy Grace. God appears to be all but forgotten.'[33] Bishop Grace has been heard to tell his worshippers: 'Never mind about God. Salvation is by Grace only. Grace has given God a vacation, and since God is on His vacation, don't worry Him. . . . If you sin against God, Grace can save you, but if you sin against Grace, God cannot save you.'[34]

This cult is distinguished by physical frenzy in which the sex motive is prominent. With aid of a piano and a drum the worshippers engage in ecstatic dancing during which in response to allusions to sex motives, the worshippers cry out, 'Daddy, you feel so good'. These emotional debauches are generally used to collect money from the members. Moreover, Grace engaged in all kinds of businesses, the products of which bore his name, as for example, Daddy Grace Toothpaste.

When Bishop Grace died his wealth was variously estimated to be from five million to twenty-five million dollars. Since he died suddenly on the West coast, the funeral *cortège* crossed the country, stopping at a number of cities for funeral services which provided occasions for wild frenzied gatherings on the part of his worshippers. He was finally buried in a large expensive mausoleum in New Bedford, Massachusetts, the scene of his first home in the United States.

Only relatively brief attention can be given to those cults which belong more specifically to the Spiritualistic group. It seems that the Spiritualist cult in Chicago was founded in New Orleans and transplanted to the North.[35] This cult flourished especially during the Great Depression. It should be noted that it borrowed its hymns from the Baptists and Methodists, and its altar candles and statues from the Catholic Church. The preachers and mediums wore colourful robes and offered heal-

33. *Ibid.*, p. 26.
34. *Ibid.*, p. 26.
35. Drake and Cayton, *op. cit.*, p. 642.

ing advice, and 'good luck' for a prayer and the price of a
candle or holy flower. The mediums claimed direct contact
with the sources of wisdom. The Spiritualist cult was differentiated from the Holiness cult by the fact that the former was not
opposed to card-playing, dancing, or 'sporting life'. It was
rumoured that it might give advice in playing the illicit lottery
game, known as 'policy' or 'the numbers'.

We come finally to two cults which are of considerable
importance because in them the Negro does not seek salvation
in the usual sense but finds an escape from his identification as a
Negro. One of these cults is the Church of God or Black Jews.[36]
The cult was founded years ago by a Negro, known as Prophet
F. S. Cherry, from 'the Deep South, which he refers to as a
place worse than hell'. He is a self-educated man who has
travelled over the world as a seaman and worked as a common
labourer all over the United States. Prophet Cherry welcomes
educated men to his church but takes a special pleasure in
ridiculing educated people and making fun of their manners
and ways of thinking. He seems to get a great deal of pleasure
from his vituperations against the clergy whom he calls 'damn
fools' and 'vultures'. On his pulpit there is always a Bible in
Yiddish and another in Hebrew since he is conversant with
these two languages. He does not wear a special dress as the
leaders of many cults, except occasionally when he appears in a
black academic gown, the sleeves having yellow stripes.

As the head of the cult Prophet Cherry appoints elders, who
may take his place in the pulpit, deacons, deaconesses and
secretaries who supervise the finances and the routine affairs of
the organization. Membership in the organization is open to
any 'black' person. While it is highly desirable that new members should have a religious experience involving a vision or
some kind of 'spirit possession', this is not a requisite for membership. This cult looks with disfavour on 'speaking in tongues'
and emotion, though holy dancing within decent limitations is
regarded as proper. There is no collection of money during
services though there is a receptacle hanging at the door for
donations as people enter the church and members are required
to pay tithes.

The sacred text of the cult is really the Talmud instead of the

36. See Fauset, *op. cit.*, Chapter IV.

Bible but the prophet always refers to the Hebrew Bible as the final authority. The members of the cult think of themselves as Black Jews and insist that the so-called Jew is a fraud. They believe in Jesus Christ but claim that he was a black man. According to them the Black People were the original inhabitants of the earth. Moreover, God is black and Jacob was black. The enslavement of the Negro and his emancipation were foretold in the Bible and the world will never be right until Black Jews occupy high places in the world. Such beliefs provide the basis of the sermons by the Prophet. After the Italians invaded Ethiopia,[37] he railed against the Pope for condoning the invasion and predicted that Hitler would drive him out of Rome. Services are held on Sunday, Wednesday, and Friday evenings and all day Saturday, which is regarded as the Sabbath or Holy Day. The members of the cult do not observe Christmas or Easter. Funerals are to be held in funeral parlours and the deceased, who can only be viewed by very close relatives, must be taken from the house as soon as possible.

In this cult, it will be noted, the Negro members have found an escape from their traditional identification and lowly status and become the first people of the earth. Even God has become black. This transformation of the Negroes is reinforced by the learning of the Hebrew language on the part of the members of the cult. The fact that they have dispensed with the Bible as the final authority and refused to observe such Christian holidays as Christmas and Easter is an indication of the extent to which they have broken with traditional Negro religion. It is also significant that death and funerals, which have been such an important part of the religious life of the Negro, are of little consequence.

The second cult, the Moorish Science Temple of America, represents an even more radical departure from the traditional religion of the Negro. Moreover, as we shall see, it takes on the character of a nationalistic religion. The founder of the Moorish Science Temple was Timothy Drew who was born in North Carolina in 1886.[38] Sometime in his life he came into contact with oriental philosophy and 'was impressed with its racial catholicity. The fruits of his research have been compressed

37. *Ibid.*, p. 39.
38. See Fauset, *op. cit.*, Chapter V.

into the Holy Koran of the Moorish Holy Temple of Science, which is not to be confused with the orthodox Mohammedan Koran.'[39] Moreover, he became obsessed with the idea that Negroes could find salvation by discovering their national origin and refuse henceforth 'to be called Negroes, black folk, coloured people, or Ethiopians' and call themselves Asiatics or specifically Moors or Moorish Americans. He began his crusade by haranguing small groups of Negroes on street corners, in tenements, and on vacant lots. To compensate for his little formal education, he possessed a certain personal magnetism and gave evidence of being sincere in his desire to help Negroes to escape from race prejudice and racial discriminations. He established his first temple in Newark, New Jersey, and as his following increased, temples were set up in Pittsburgh, Detroit, and cities in the South. But his major achievement was the establishment of a temple in Chicago.

Hundreds of Negroes in Chicago flocked to the new leader, who had become known as Noble Drew Ali. They believed that the change in identification from Negro to Asiatic would bring salvation. The members were given a large calling card which bore the inscription: a replica of star and crescent with ISLAM beneath it, a replica of clasped hands with UNITY above it, and a replica of circled '7' with ALLAH beneath it.[40] Beneath this was the statement that the card represented their nationality and identification card, that the cult honoured all divine prophets, Jesus, Mohammed, Buddha, and Confucius, and that the bearer was a Moslem under the Divine laws of the Holy Koran of Mecca, Love, Truth, Peace, Freedom, and Justice. There was added: 'I AM A CITIZEN OF THE U.S.A.' Negroes who carried this card believed that the mere showing of the card would restrain white men if they would be inclined to disturb or harm Negroes. In fact, the members of the cult became so aggressive and insulting in their behaviour towards whites that it was necessary for the Noble Drew Ali to admonish them against such behaviour. As the cult grew, some Negroes with education joined the organization and attempted to exploit the members by selling 'herbs, magical charms, and potions, and literature pertaining to the cult'. As the internal strife increased,

39. *Ibid.*, p. 41.
40. See Fauset, *op. cit.*, p. 42.

one of these would-be leaders was killed and Noble Drew Ali was arrested for murder, though he was not in Chicago at the time. He died under mysterious circumstances after being released from jail under bond and was awaiting trial. After the death of Noble Drew Ali, the cult split into a number of sects with some claiming that they were following him in his re-incarnation.

Something needs to be said about the beliefs and ritual and practices of the cult. The members of the various sects which have split off from the parent body live according to the teachings which have been divulged to Noble Drew Ali and are contained in the Holy Koran.[41] Jesus figures largely in the Koran but Allah is God and He ordained his Prophet, Noble Drew Ali, to divulge his secrets to the dark folk of America. The charter of the Moorish Science Temple is supposed to have come from the 'great capital empire of Egypt'. Negro (black) signifies death and coloured something painted. Therefore, the term Moorish-American must be used. In their religious services, which meet promptly and are dismissed promptly, the contents of the Holy Koran are expounded to the members. During the services, which are extremely quiet, men and women are segregated. ' "Christmas" is observed on January fifth, the anniversary of the day when the prophet, Noble Drew Ali, was reincarnated.' Members greet each other, the right hand upraised and the palm turned out, with the words 'Peace' and 'Islam'. There are a number of taboos, including the prohibition of the use of meat and eggs, the use of intoxicants, attendance at European games and the straightening of the hair.

The Moorish Science Temple represents the most radical secularization of Negro religion or of the Negro church in the city. While the regular denominations have increasingly focused attention upon the solution of the Negro's problems or his salvation in this world, they have the essentials of traditional Negro religion. Likewise, in the 'storefront' churches, there is an attempt among the lower class to re-create in the urban environment a type of religious organization in which they can find

41. See Fauset, *op. cit.*, pp. 46 ff. Fauset was able to secure only through an ex-member, and through the neglect of another member, access to the Holy Koran. He felt that he would be violating a trust to divulge all the contents of the Holy Koran. Footnote, p. 45.

warm and sympathetic association and status. In a sense these changes in the traditional religious life of the Negro are an attempt to escape from the hard conditions under which Negroes live in the cities and to find a meaning for living. This escape is most marked in those cults in which the Negro becomes a new person, as in the cult of the Black Jews and the Moorish Science Temple. This latter cult is especially important both because it provides the Negro with a kind of national identification and because of its extremely secular outlook. This secular outlook is becoming common among the masses who are without church affiliation and scorn the saying which was once popular among the humble masses: 'Take the world and give me Jesus.' It is also evident among those who though still affiliated with churches do not trust to the Providence of God alone, but hope that the 'numbers', or chance, will bring them security or fortune. Among those who depend upon chance there are many who have a purely hedonistic outlook on life and organize their lives around 'good-timing'. But most of them aspire to middle-class ideals and want to 'get ahead'. All of this is the result of the uprooting of the Negro from his traditional social organization in which the Negro church was the most important institution and set the patterns of behaviour and thought and the values for the majority of Negroes.

CHAPTER 5

The Negro Church and Assimilation

The Walls Came Tumbling Down

I N the last chapter we have studied the transformations which have occurred in the Negro church and in the religion of Negroes as the result of urbanization. We have seen how the migrations of Negroes to cities have tended to uproot the traditional organization of the Negro community and changed the outlook of Negroes. As the result of the social disorganization of Negro life there has been a reorganization of life on a different basis in order to meet the demands of the city. Life in the cities of the North has brought a larger measure of freedom from racial prejudice and discriminations which had characterized race relations in the South. This new freedom has enabled Negroes to enter more into the mainstream of American life. Since this new freedom has been due partly to broad changes in the economic and social organization of American life, the Negro in the South benefited from these changes. The success which Negroes have achieved in breaking down racial barriers has been due partly to their own efforts. They have carried on a constant struggle in the courts and they have influenced to some extent public opinion. As the mid-century drew to a close a distinguished white woman, who had been associated with their struggle, could look back at the success which Negroes had made in breaking through racial barriers and say in the words of the well-known Negro spiritual, 'the walls came tumbling down'.[1]

However, as the racial barriers are broken down and Negroes increasingly enter into the mainstream of American life, the traditional organization of Negro life is constantly being undermined. The so-called process of integration, which is only an

---

1. Joshua fit de battle of Jericho,
   Jericho, Jericho,
   Joshua fit de battle of Jericho,
   And de walls came tumbling down.

Mary White Ovington, *The Walls Came Tumbling Down* NewYork, (1947).

initial stage in the assimilation of Negroes into American society, does not have the same effect on all parts of the social structure of the Negro community. The extent and the nature of the participation of Negroes in the wider American community is determined first by their class position. Negroes in the Black Belt or rural counties in the South where they constitute 50 per cent or more of the population are still almost completely isolated from the main currents of American culture. Although lower-class Negroes in cities, who include those engaged in domestic and personal services and those employed as unskilled labourers, have more contacts with American life, they are still more or less confined to the Negro community. As Negro workers acquire skills and become members of labour unions, they begin to enter into the mainstream of American life. This is, of course, more characteristic of Negro workers in the North than of those in the South. Many Negroes in the North who are employed as white-collar workers and in technical and professional occupations enter even more fully into the main currents of American society. Not only does their work enable them to share more fully in American culture but they associate more freely with their white fellow workers than any other section of the Negro population.

The second factor and a factor of equal importance, which determines the nature and extent of the participation of Negroes in the wider American community, is their own institutional life. The system of racial segregation in the United States has resulted in an almost complete duplication of the institutions of the American community within the Negro community.[2] We shall begin by considering those institutions which embody the secular interests of Negroes. As Negroes have moved from the world of the folk, they have established insurance companies and banks which have a purely secular end. These institutions are becoming a part of the different associations of insurance companies and banks and they are subject to state supervision. Then there are many other kinds of business enterprises, many of which cater especially to the personal and other needs of Negroes, and thus supply services often refused by white establishments. Negroes are expected to patronize these various so-

2. See Frazier, *The Negro in the United States*, Part 3, 'The Negro Community and Its Institutions'.

called 'Negro' businesses because of 'racial loyalty'. There is a National Negro Business League and numerous Negro chambers of commerce. Among the more successful Negro businesses should be included the Negro weekly newspapers which have circulations running into the hundreds of thousands.

Then there are certain cultural institutions among which are included the various secret fraternal organizations such as the Masons, Odd Fellows, and the Elks. In this group we would also include the various college Greek letter societies for men and women. Although they would not qualify as institutions, there are numerous social clubs which may be considered along with the cultural institutions. The most important cultural institution is, of course, the Negro church. It embodies, as we have seen, the cultural traditions of Negroes to a far greater extent than any other institution.

As 'the walls of segregation tumble down', it is the institutions which embody the secular interests of Negroes which are being undermined more rapidly than those representing their cultural interests. As white establishments cater to the personal needs of Negroes there is less need for what is known as 'Negro' businesses to supply such services. Moreover, as the large corporations and other so-called white business enterprises employ Negroes in all capacities, there is less need for an association of people engaged in 'Negro' businesses. Likewise, as white newspapers carry more news concerning Negroes and employ Negro journalists, the Negro newspapers decline in circulation as the foreign language newspapers have done. Although schools are cultural institutions, the segregated Negro public schools and state colleges will become less important.

The situation is different in regard to the cultural institutions within the Negro community. There are some privately supported Negro educational institutions with deeply rooted traditions in Negro life that resist the trend towards the integration of the Negro. On the other hand, as Negro professors are increasingly taken on the faculties of so-called white colleges and universities and Negro students are admitted to such institutions, Negroes are joining the mainstream of American life. When one comes to the Negro church which is the most important cultural institution created by Negroes, one encounters the most important institutional barrier to integration and the assimilation of Negroes. White churches may open their doors to Negroes and a few Negro ministers may be invited to become pastors of white churches; the masses of Negroes continue, nevertheless, to attend the Negro churches and the Negro church as an institution continues to function as an important element in the organized social life of Negroes.

The Church is no Longer a Refuge

The strength of the Negro church as a barrier to the integration of Negroes into the main currents of American life should not be overestimated, especially since the process of integration has not progressed very far. Moreover, it is necessary to differentiate the situation in the North from that in the South. In the South the Negro has scarcely begun his struggle to participate in the secular and public institutions of the American community. On the other hand, in the border states and in the North there is much larger participation of Negroes in the secular and public institutions of the American community. In the South the lives of Negroes still revolve about the activities of the Negro community. Even where they gain entrance into labour unions, they are excluded from the 'social' activities of these organizations. In the North Negroes are included increasingly in the 'social' activities of the various labour unions. Nevertheless, in the North the proliferation of organizations which provide for the 'social' needs of Negroes indicate the extent to which Negroes are still outsiders, so to speak. Moreover, the ecological or spatial segregation of Negroes, which is often the result of impersonal economic and social forces rather than prejudice and discrimination, tends to maintain the separate institutions of the Negro community. The church is the most important of these institutions in which the masses of Negroes find a refuge within white society which treats them with condescension if not contempt.

But the Negro church can no longer serve as a refuge as it did in the past when the majority of Negroes lived in the South under a system of racial segregation and the majority of the Negroes in the South lived in rural areas. Willy-nilly Negroes are drawn into the complex social organization of the American community. This is necessary for mere survival. Recognizing the need for a more complex social organization to serve the

needs of urbanized Negroes and at the same time taking cogni-
zance of the fact that Negroes were still excluded from labour
unions, a Negro sociologist proposed that the Negro church,
being the largest organized unit of Negro life, incorporate some
of the functions of the new forms of organized social life which
are required in the city.[3] It is apparent, however, that this proposal was impractical since the Negro church could not perform the functions of the new types of associations necessary to
life in the city.

It was inevitable that the Negro should be drawn into the
organized forms of social life in the urban environment. As a
consequence, the Negro church has lost much of its influence
as an agency of social control. Its supervision over the marital
and family life of Negroes has declined. The church has ceased
to be the chief means of economic co-operation. New avenues
have been opened to all kinds of business ventures in which
secular ends and values are dominant. The church is no longer
the main arena for political activities which was the case when
Negroes were disfranchised in the South. Negro political
leaders have to compete with the white political leaders in the
'machine' politics of the cities. In a word, the Negroes have
been forced into competition with whites in most areas of social
life and their church can no longer serve as a refuge within the
American community.

We have seen how Negroes in the established denominational
churches developed secular interests in order to deal with race
prejudice and discriminations to which they are exposed when
the 'walls of segregation come tumbling down'. We have seen
how lower-class Negroes have reacted to the cold impersonal
environment of the city and of the large denominational churches
by joining the 'storefront' churches and the various cults. These
all represented their reaction to the crumbling traditional organization of Negro life as Negroes are increasingly cast afloat in
the main stream of American life where they are still outsiders.

The Gospel Singers

Although the lower strata in the Negro community do not
participate to the same extent as the upper strata in the main

3. See the proposal of Dr. George E. Haynes of the Federal Council of
Churches, quoted in Drake and Cayton, *Black Metropolis*, p. 683.

currents of American life, they are nevertheless increasingly assimilating the manners and customs of American society. There is thus achieved a certain external conformity to the patterns of American culture.[4] They continue to be influenced in their thinking and especially in their feelings and sentiments by the social heritage of the Negro which is represented by the Spirituals and religious orientation towards the world contained in the Spirituals. The masses of Negroes may increasingly criticize the church and their ministers, but they cannot escape from their heritage. They may develop a more secular outlook on life and complain that the church and the ministers are not sufficiently concerned with the problems of the Negro race,[5] yet they find in their religious heritage an opportunity to satisfy their deepest emotional yearnings.

Out of the revolt of the lower strata against the church and the growing secularization of Negro religion there has come an accommodation between traditional Negro religion and the new outlook of Negroes in the new American environment. This accommodation is symbolized by the Gospel Singers. The songs which the Gospel Singers sing have been described as a compound of 'elements found in the old tabernacle songs, the Negro Spirituals and the blues'.[6] Since the Negro has become urbanized, there has been an amazing rise and spread of 'gospel singing'. This has been attributed, and correctly so, to the fact that, 'As Negro churches have become more European in decorum and programme, the great mass of less Europeanized Negroes began to look elsewhere for full vented religious expressions in music and preaching.'[7] The important fact is that although the Gospel Singers have gone outside the church for a congenial form of religious expression, they nevertheless remain in the church and are a part of the church. Recently when a Gospel Singer died and her funeral was held in a large Baptist church in the Nation's Capital, it was reported that 13,000

---

4. Cf. 'Racial Assimilation in Secondary Groups', in Robert E. Park, *Race and Culture* (Glencoe, Ill., 1950), Chapter 16.

5. See Drake and Cayton, *op. cit.*, pp. 650–4, concerning the rebellion of the lower classes against the church.

6. Arna Bontemps, 'Rock, Church, Rock', in Sylvester C. Watkins (ed.), *Anthology of American Negro Literature* (New York, 1944), p. 431.

7. Willis Laurence James, 'The Romance of the Negro Folk Cry in America', *Phylon*, Vol. XVI (1955), p. 23.

persons viewed her remains, a thousand persons jammed the church, and another thousand lined the sidewalks outside the church. Dozens of gospel-singing groups came from neighbouring areas and as far away as Pennsylvania and Illinois. The white owner of a broadcasting company flew from Ohio to attend the funeral. Between 150 and 200 cars accompanied the body to the cemetery.[8]

More important still for us here is the fact that the Gospel Singers symbolize something that is characteristic of Negro religion from the standpoint of assimilation. Some of the so-called advanced Negro churches resented these gospel singers and refused to permit them to sing within their churches. They have gradually become more tolerant and let down the bars as the Gospel Singers have acquired status and acceptance within the white world. Such well-known gospel singers as Mahalia Jackson, Rosetta Thorpe, and the Ward Sisters have been accepted as 'artists'. The Gospel Singer not only sings to the Negro world but sings to the white world. One of the famous Ward Sisters stated that the gospel singing is popular because '. . . it fills a vacuum in people's lives. For people who work hard and make little money it offers a promise that things will be better in the life to come.'[9] She was thinking, of course, of Negroes but the Gospel Singers sing to white America as well. This is indicated by their hold on the record industry and their popularity on radio and television programmes.

Gospel singing has, of course, become commercialized and that is another indication of the relation of Negro religious life to assimilation. It indicates in a sense the terms on which the Negro is being assimilated. Moreover, white men in the South are beginning to imitate the Negro Gospel Singers. And Negro gospel singing is often featured as a part of the programmes on television. Thus, the religious folk-songs of the Negro are becoming secularized despite the fact that the singing of them

8. See *Washington Afro-American*, 5 April, 1960, for featured article on front page concerning death and funeral of Thelma Greene, at which a member of the Robert Martin Singers of Chicago sang a solo, 'God Specializes', causing a number of persons to faint and to be carried out by nurses.

9. Interview with Clara Mae Ward in Winston-Salem, who claims she is only gospel singer ever to have visited the Holy Land. 'Singing for Sinners', *News Week*, Vol. 50 (2 September, 1957), p. 86.

in secular entertainment is a concession to the so-called religious revival in the United States. The Gospel Singers, then, unlike the cults, do not represent a complete break with the religious traditions of the Negro. They represent or symbolize the attempt of the Negro to utilize his religious heritage in order to come to terms with changes in his own institutions as well as the problems of the world of which he is a part.

In a sense, therefore, the attempts of the Negro to resist segregation in the sit-down strikes in the South represent the same falling back upon his religious heritage in time of crisis. This movement on the part of Negro students in the South is supposed to be based upon the non-violent resistance movement of Gandhi.[10] Some of its intellectual leaders like the Reverend Martin Luther King may use Gandhi's non-violent resistance as an ideological justification of the movement, but Gandhism as a philosophy and a way of life is completely alien to the Negro and has nothing in common with the social heritage of the Negro. As Negro students go forth singing the Spirituals or the Gospel hymns when they engage in sit-down strikes or sing their Gospel songs in response to violence, they are behaving in accordance with the religious heritage of the Negro.

Then there is another aspect of this movement which needs to be considered in relation to the changes in the religion of the Negro. Because of the improvement in their economic conditions, an increasing number of Negro students are able to attend the colleges for Negroes in the South. They are being drawn from those strata in the Negro population closest to the rural background and who, therefore, are closest to the folk heritage of the Negro. Education, or more specially the opportunity to attend college, is the most important factor enabling Negroes to achieve middle-class status. Moreover, the leaders of this movement have seen something of the world because of their army or other experiences, or their parents have had similar experiences. In their revolt against the racial discrimination they must fall back upon the only vital social heritage that has meaning for them and that social heritage is the religious heritage represented by the Spirituals which are becoming secularized.

10. See 'The Revolt of Negro Youth', *Ebony* (May, 1960).

The Religion of the New Middle Class

We have already seen in the last chapter how the Negro church and Negro religion have been affected by the new class structure which is emerging among Negroes in cities, especially in the North. Here we are interested in the religious outlook of the new Negro middle class which has become important among Negroes during the past twenty years or so. It is this class whose outward appearance and standards of behaviour approximate most nearly the norms of the white American society. Moreover, Negroes who have achieved middle-class status participate more largely than any other element in American life. It is for this reason that we shall focus attention upon the new middle class in studying the changes in the religious life of Negroes as they are related to the assimilation of Negroes into American society.

The growing importance of the new middle class in the Negro community is due to the continual differentiation of the population along occupational lines. Therefore, the new middle class is composed almost entirely of those persons who derive their incomes from services rendered as white-collar workers and as professional men and women. Despite the dreams of Negro leaders, fostered by the National Negro Business League at the turn of the century, that Negroes would organize big industries and large financial undertakings, Negroes have not become captains of industry nor even managers of large corporations. So-called 'Negro' business continues to consist mainly of small retail stores catering to the personal needs of Negroes. There are a small number of insurance companies, small banks, and newspapers which constitute their larger business enterprises. The owners and managers of these enterprises constitute the upper layer of the middle class while the increasing number of Negroes in skilled occupations constitute its lowest stratum. For reasons which have been indicated, in the North and West about 25 per cent of the Negro population is able to maintain middle-class standards while in the South only about 12 per cent are in this position.

The new Negro middle class is a new phenomenon in the Negro community because it has a different economic base and a different social heritage from the relatively small middle class which had become differentiated from the masses of Negroes by the first decade of this century.[11] This older middle class was an 'aristocratic' *élite* in a sense because its social status and pre-eminence were based upon white ancestry and family and its behaviour was modelled after the genteel tradition of the Old South. The upper layer derived their incomes from land but the majority of the members of the '*élite*' were employed in a large variety of occupations including positions as trusted retainers in white families. The new middle class has a different occupational basis and occupation is one of the important factors in determining status.

Since the opening of the century there had been a faith among middle-class Negroes in 'Negro' business as a means of solving their social as well as economic problems. This faith was somewhat as follows: as Negroes became businessmen they would accumulate capital and give employment to Negroes and once Negroes possessed wealth, white men would respect them and accord them equality. The new middle class has accepted without the critical attitude which experience should have given them, the faith in 'Negro' business as a way to social and economic salvation.

Since the emergence of the new middle class involves the rise of the more ambitious and energetic elements among the masses of Negroes to middle-class status, this new class does not possess the genteel tradition of the older middle class. This new class is largely without social roots except the traditions of the Negro folk represented in the Spirituals. But as these Negroes rise to middle-class status they reject the folk heritage and seek to slough off any reminders of their folk inheritance. However, since their rise to the middle-class status has enabled them to marry into families with the genteel tradition of the old middle class, there is often a confusion of 'aristocratic' and folk values. It is for this reason that many middle-class Negroes exhibit in their manners and behaviour the characteristics of both a peasant and a gentleman. Among this new class there is much confusion as to standards of behaviour and beliefs. There is a constant striving to acquire money in order to engage in conspicuous consumption which provides the outward signs of status and

11. E. Franklin Frazier, 'The Negro Middle Class and Desegregation', *Social Problems*, Vol. IV (April 1957), pp. 291–301.

conformity to white American standards. They all possess the same goal, which is acceptance into the white community and they all profess, at least, a desire to be integrated into the white community.

Integration for the majority of middle-class Negroes means the loss of racial identity or an escape from the lowly status of Negroes and the contempt of whites. With integration they began to remove as much as possible from the names of their various organizations anything that would identify them as Negroes. This even extended to their church organizations. The Colored Methodist Episcopal Church became the 'Christian' Methodist Episcopal Church. It is significant, however, that when the middle-class leaders in the African Methodist Episcopal Church attempted to take 'African' out of the name and substitute the word 'American', there was a revolt on the part of the masses who demanded that 'African' be retained. This incident is indicative of the general attitude of the middle class towards the African background of the Negro. While there is some outward profession of pride in African independence and identification with Africa, the middle class rejects identification with Africa and wants above all to be accepted as 'just Americans'. It was the new middle class which was rising to importance in the 1920s that was most bitterly opposed to the Garvey Movement which had as its goal the identification of Negroes with Africa and African interests.[12] Middle-class Negroes seize upon identification with Africa only as a means of compensating for their feeling of inferiority and improving their status in the eyes of American whites.

Despite the fact that middle-class Negroes conform to the standards of whites and accept without question the values of American society, they are still rejected by the white world. They feel this rejection more keenly than lower-class Negroes who participate less in the white man's world and conform to the standards of their own separate world. Moreover, because of their position, middle-class Negroes have an ambivalent attitude towards their identification as Negroes. On the one hand, they resent the slightest aspersion upon Negroes. When placed in competition with whites they have feelings of inadequacy and when they find themselves in close association with whites they

12. See Frazier, *The Negro in the United States*, pp. 528–31.

have feelings of insecurity though they may clamour for integration into the white world.[13] They are status seekers in a double sense; they strive to keep up with the expectations of their class in the Negro community and they seek or hope to gain status in the white world. In order to maintain high standards of consumption often both husband and wife work but they constantly complain of the 'rat race' to maintain life as they would live it. They live frustrated lives despite their efforts to compensate for their feelings of inferiority and insecurity. They have little time for leisure and the enjoyment of what they call the 'cultural' things of life. As a matter of fact, they have little appreciation of music or art and they read very little since reading has not become a tradition in the new middle class.

Their ambiguous position in American society together with their recent rise to middle-class status are reflected in the religious behaviour and attitudes of middle-class Negroes. There is first a tendency for middle-class Negroes to sever their affiliation with the Baptist and Methodist churches and join the Presbyterian, Congregational, and Episcopal churches. The middle-class Negroes who continue their affiliation with the Baptist and Methodist churches choose those churches with intelligent ministers and a relatively large middle-class membership. As a consequence there is a solid core of the Negro middle class that continues to be affiliated with the Negro church. However, middle-class Negroes continue their affiliation with the Negro church for a number of reasons. Their families may have been associated with the churches and the churches which they have known since childhood provide a satisfying form of religious worship. Although many middle-class Negroes continue to be affiliated with the church, the church is no longer the centre of social life for them as for the lower class. They are members of professional and business associations and Greek letter fraternal organizations, though 'social' clubs constitute the vast majority of these other forms of organized social activities. Some are thus able to satisfy their striving for status outside the church. But for others it is necessary to leave the Baptist and Methodist churches and join the Presbyterian, Congregational, and Episcopal churches in order to satisfy the desire for status.

13. E. Franklin Frazier, *Black Bourgeoisie* (Glencoe, Ill., 1957), pp. 216 ff.

The striving for status and the searching for a means to escape from a frustrated existence is especially marked among the middle-class Negroes who cannot find a satisfactory life within the regular Negro church organization. This probably accounts for the fact that during the past two decades middle-class Negroes have been joining the Catholic church.[14] Sometimes they send their children to Catholic schools where they will receive a discipline not provided in the public schools for Negroes. Very often after joining the Catholic church with the expectation that they will escape from their status as Negroes, they find that they are still defined as Negroes by whites. Some middle-class Negroes in their seeking to find escape from the Negro identification have gone from the Catholic church to the Christian Science church and then to the Bahaist church. Moreover, there is a tendency among middle-class Negroes to be attracted to Moral Re-armament, hoping that they would find a group in which they could lose completely their identification as Negroes and escape from their feelings of inferiority and insecurity. A small intellectual fringe among middle-class Negroes have affiliated with the Unitarian church. But some of them may still attend more or less surreptitiously the Methodist and Baptist churches on Friday nights.

This type of dual church affiliation is more characteristic of Negro professional men who affiliate with churches mainly for social and professional reasons. Some professional Negroes affiliate with a church which their friends or middle-class Negroes attend, and at the same time affiliate with churches attended by the lower class who are their clients. They are representative of the growing number of middle-class Negroes who have a purely secular outlook on the world. Some of them express contempt for religion and do not attend church though they may pretend to have some church affiliation. Since they have neither an intellectual heritage nor a social philosophy except a crude opportunism which enables them to get by in the white man's world, they may turn to all forms of superstition. This is because they are still haunted by the fears and

14. The recent increase during the past twenty years in the number, which remains relatively small, of lower-class Negroes in the Catholic church has been due to aid provided them during the *Depression years* and the better educational facilities, as compared with the public schools, provided them by the Catholic church.

beliefs which are a part of their folk heritage. They are often interested in 'spiritual' and 'psychic' phenomena. Very often the real religious feelings and faith of middle-class Negroes are expressed in their obsession with poker and other forms of gambling.[15]

The religious behaviour and outlook of the middle-class Negroes is a reflection of their ambiguous position as Negroes rise to middle-class status and become increasingly integrated into the American community. To the extent that they are becoming really assimilated into American society, they are being beset by the religious dilemmas and doubts of the white middle-class Americans. On the other hand, for the masses of Negroes, the Negro church continues to be a refuge, though increasingly less of a refuge, in a hostile white world.

15. See *Black Bourgeoisie*, pp. 209 ff.

Conclusion

I N this concluding chapter, we shall summarize the main points brought out in this study. The important role of religion in the social organization of American Negroes has been due to the conditions under which Negroes were introduced into the New World and to their subordination and relative social isolation in American society. No one can say what would have been the role of religion among Negroes if they had not been isolated from the main currents of American life. But under the circumstances of their subordination and isolation in American society it is difficult to imagine organized social life among Negroes without the important role of the religion and the Negro church. The Negroes were practically stripped of their social heritage and their traditional social organization was destroyed as the result of the manner in which they were enslaved and became the labour force in the plantation economy. They did not possess a historical tradition and whatever memories of their African culture were preserved through oral transmission lost their meaning when there was no longer a social organization to sustain them.

There was one element in their African heritage that was able to survive capture in Africa and the 'middle passage'—dancing, the most primitive form of religious expression. The slaves were encouraged to dance during the 'middle passage' and in the West Indies the slaves were forced to dance as a part of the breaking-in process. In the 'shout-songs' on the Sea Islands off the coast of South Carolina and Georgia one may discover the remnants of the African religious heritage. However, no African religious cults became established on American soil. The whites did everything possible to suppress these 'heathenish' practices. The Established Church with its emphasis upon a knowledge of the catechism for baptism and with its religious ritual requiring decorum did not make much progress among the slaves. It was only with the coming of the Baptist and Methodist missionaries that the slaves found a form of religion in which they could give expression to their deepest emotions. The adventitious gatherings in which tribeless men and women without even the bonds of kinship could find an ephemeral solidarity became regular meetings for religious services and a new bond of cohesion was established in the New World. Not only was a new bond with their fellow slaves established but as they joined in the religious services of their white masters their moral isolation in the white world began to break down.

So far as the slaves were permitted some autonomy in their religious life, there came into existence what might be called an 'invisible institution' of the Negro church. At the same time the Negroes who were free before the Civil War left the white Methodist and Baptist church organizations in which they had a subordinate status and set up their own churches. After Emancipation the 'invisible institution' of the Negro church was absorbed by the institutional churches which the Negroes who were free before the Civil War had established. There was some conflict between the two elements because the former slaves preferred a more primitive form of worship and continued the religious tradition represented in the Spirituals. Nevertheless, the two elements fused in church organizations which became the major form of organized social life among Negroes. For the masses of Negroes who were segregated from the mainstream of American life, the church communities in the South became a sort of nation within a nation.

Out of the church organizations grew other forms of organized activities among the Negroes who were free before the Civil War. After Emancipation the enlarged church organizations played an even more important role in the organization of the Negro community. They were responsible not only for economic co-operation for the purpose of erecting and buying churches, but they also provided the incentive for the pooling of the meagre economic means of Negroes for mutual assistance and insurance companies. It was almost solely through the Negro church organizations that the initiative on the part of Negroes in securing an education and building educational institutions was expressed. Inasmuch as Negroes were excluded from political participation in the American community at large, the Negro church organization became the most important arena for political life among Negroes. It was in the contests carried on within these organizations that Negroes struggled for power and position and the members could exercise some choice in the selection of men to govern them. Thus, the Negro church organizations became the most effective agencies of social control among Negroes in their relatively isolated social world. And as far as the outside hostile white world was concerned, the Negro churches became a refuge or helped Negroes to become accommodated to their inferior status.

The urbanization of Negroes on a large scale, beginning with the First World War, has brought about a transformation of the Negro church and changed the outlook of Negroes upon the world and their place in the world. There has been a secularization of outlook and Negro churches have not failed to reflect this change in outlook. The regularly established Negro churches placed less emphasis upon salvation after death and directed their activities increasingly to the economic, social, and political problems of Negroes in this world. The reorganization of the religious life of Negroes in the urban environment has been influenced largely by the new class structure of Negro communities, especially in the North, which is the result of the increasing occupational differentiation of the Negro population. Among the upper strata there has been a shift from the Baptist and Methodist churches to the Presbyterian, Episcopalian, and Congregational churches. The lower strata who became lost in the impersonal atmosphere of the large city churches and longed for the intimate association of the small churches of the South where they could give free rein to their emotions, have sought a more congenial religious worship in the 'storefront' churches. A more important change among the lower strata has expressed itself in the various holiness cults which seek a return to a primitive form of Christianity. The most radical deviation from the traditional religious orientation of Negroes has been in those cults which enable the Negro to escape from his racial identification and exalt secular nationalistic aims.

Since the urbanization of the Negro population has been due to broader changes in the economic and social organization of American life, it has been responsible for the increasing integration of Negroes into the mainstream of American civilization. As a result of the increasing integration, the social organization of Negro communities has been changed. And since the church has been the main form or focus of organized social life among Negroes it has been affected by integration. One of the consequences is that the church is no longer the refuge for Negroes that it was formerly. In response to the changing position of the Negro churches has been the emergence of the Gospel Singers, whose gospel songs express the deep religious feelings of the Negro masses who are increasingly exposed to life in the American community. They sing their gospel songs which are a blend of sacred and secular music, not only in Negro churches but address them to the white world as well which is beginning to sing them too.

One of the most important results of the new stratification of the Negro community has been the emergence of a relatively large new middle class, which at the same time is the most advanced element in the process of integration. Although the new middle class seeks identification with and acceptance by the white middle class, it is rejected by the latter. Moreover, the new middle class has rejected the Negro heritage, including the religious heritage. As a consequence this class occupies an ambiguous position in relation to both Negroes and whites. In its efforts to escape from its frustrations and dilemmas the new Negro middle class sometimes abandons religion altogether but more often shifts its affiliation from church to church or from one religious fad to another. Sometimes they became interested in 'spiritual' and 'psychic' phenomena and other forms of superstitition including dependence upon 'luck' and 'chance'. However, to the extent that they are truly assimilated in the culture of the white middle class, they experience the same religious doubts and dilemmas as whites of the same class.

The important role of religion and the Negro church in the social organization of the American Negroes has been due to the restricted participation of Negroes in American society. And as a consequence the Negro church has left its imprint upon practically every aspect of Negro life. The Negro church has provided the pattern for the organization of mutual aid societies and insurance companies. It has provided the pattern of Negro fraternal organizations and Greek letter societies. It has provided the pattern of administration and control of the Negro schools so far as they have been under the control of Negroes. Since, as we have seen, the pattern of control and organization of the Negro church has been authoritarian, with a strong man in a dominant position, the same pattern has characterized other Negro organizations. The petty tyrants in the Negro churches have their counterparts in practically all other Negro organizations. As a consequence, Negroes have had little education in democratic processes. Moreover, the Negro church and Negro religion have cast a shadow over the entire intellectual life of Negroes and have been responsible for the so-called backwardness of American Negroes. Sometimes an ignorant preacher backed by the white community has been able to intimidate Negro scholars and subvert the true aim of an educational institution. It is only as a few Negro individuals have been able to escape from the stifling domination of the church that they have been able to develop intellectually and in the field of art. This development is only being achieved on a broader scale to the extent that Negroes are being integrated into the institutions of the American community and as the social organization of the Negro community, in which the church is the dominant element, crumbles as the 'walls of segregation come tumbling down'.

INDEX

INDEX

25447

Frazier, E. F.
The Negro church in America